A Pair of Sparkly Sneakers

A Mother's Journey to Inner Wisdom

Nicole Olson

ISBN:
978-0-9885352-0-6

DEDICATION

For Thomas, whose sparkle lights my way.
-Nicole

For Dayna, who taught us unschooling, and
helped to make my life a whole lot better.
-Thomas

CONTENTS

ACKNOWLEDGMENTS

I have been privileged to live a life filled with deep friendships that have shaped and molded me from my earliest years. I am so grateful for all of them, but there are a few individuals who were instrumental in helping me along this particular journey...

The talented, dedicated professionals at GSNS, who gave unreservedly in order to support our family during the stormy times.

Dr. Beth, who gently and quietly helped to restore Thomas when the storms subsided.

Adele, who opened her home and her heart to my family at the very beginning of our journey, as she has done for countless others.

Eileen, whose friendship came into my life at just the right moment, and whose passion for the unschooling life ignited my own.

The beautiful families who make up my Village. They support, encourage and inspire me every day, and truly embody the adage for which they are named.

Julie, my cheerleader from afar, who generously

lent me her expertise, kept me smiling through the ups and downs of the process, and inspired me with the brilliant light of her being, which rivals the sun itself.

My aunt, Debra Nelson, whose editorial advice added sensitivity and dignity to this story, and whose unflagging support across the decades has nurtured my spirit.

My friend and mentor, Dayna, whose encouragement and support transformed my family, and made me the mom and unschooling advocate that I am today. It is truly inspiring to witness the way she has woven this life of freedom into a tapestry so powerful in its beauty that it transforms lives all around the world.

My dad, for whom I earned "strong A's" and from whom I learned wisdom and the value of the written word.

My mom, who made this journey beside me every step of the way, lending her support, insight and assistance. I would not be the mother I am if I had not been her daughter first.

My husband, who believed long before I did that I had a story to tell, and without whom I could not have written this. I'm so thankful to be leading this amazing life with him at my side. I am truly blessed.

My children, who show me the beauty of living an extraordinary life, and who have brought me more joy than words can express.

1 PLEASE REPORT TO THE PRINCIPLE'S OFFICE

I pulled into the school parking lot, cut the ignition, and tried to martial my resources for what lay ahead. I was there to collect my son – just barely five years old – from the principal's office, where he'd been sent for throwing snowballs. It was not the first time my little boy had landed in the office. But it would be the last.

I took a deep breath, steadying myself for what I'd come to do. I found myself thinking back, retracing the steps that had brought us here to this moment when everything would change.

It was not the first change we'd faced as a family – not by a long shot. But it would become the one change we chose to define us – to defy all the other labels that had been so haphazardly thrust upon us.

I drew in one last, shaky breath and made my way into the school, bypassing the principal's office, turning sharply to the right, down the hall that would take me to my son's classroom. I'd attended this school myself as a child, and each step evoked vivid memories; the squeak of sneakers on the dark maroon tiles as we'd line up for lunch, the faded brown door to my first-ever classroom, the stairs leading down to the mysterious room in the basement where the art teacher fired up her kiln.

I had liked school well enough – or so I had thought – back in those elementary days, and school had certainly liked me. I was a quiet, eager to please, precocious student. The kind of student that teachers silently blessed as they dealt with the loudmouthed bully, the Chatty Cathy who wouldn't buckle down, or the hopeless Bullfrogs reading group, comprised of the most inept readers.

A teacher's dream, that's what my fearless leaders always reported to my parents at conference time. *Wish we had a class full of students just like her!* My mother would float home, thrilled with such laudable news, while my father would jokingly grill me as to whether my A's were "strong" A's, or just squeaking-by ones.

A teacher's dream. It's what I'd always been. It's what I'd always assumed my children would be. Yet here I was, on my way to meet with my son's special education teacher about the nightmare he had become.

2 THE PERFECT STORM

Life with Thomas had started out as a dream come true. At thirty-one, I had been more than ready to bid farewell to my teaching career and devote myself to full time motherhood. It had always been my fondest wish, my deepest desire. Before he was conceived, I'd already taken a parenting course not once, but *twice*. Armed with my background in education, my parenting classes under my belt, and an impressive array of "how-to" books lining my bookshelves, I was pretty confident that I'd be a great mom, and that my son and I would have an idyllic relationship.

And idyllic it was – despite a rocky delivery, despite the intense sleep deprivation that's impossible to grasp ahead of time, despite the sometimes opposing views my husband and I discovered we held about child-rearing. It was a wild and intense love affair, into which I threw myself headlong. Thomas was a gentle little soul, full of joy. How he loved to laugh! He was physically advanced, always reaching his milestones well ahead of most of his peers. He was highly verbal as well, with a truly impressive vocabulary for one so young. For 23 months, Thomas and I ate, slept and breathed each other pretty much every moment of his precious little life, and the vast majority of those moments were filled with bliss.

Things started to change about two weeks before Thomas's second birthday, when we received the jolting news that I was pregnant with twins. *Twins?* I couldn't seem to comprehend it. We had planned the pregnancy, and I was excited about it, albeit a bit anxious about how another baby would impact my relationship with Thomas. But twins were not in the plan - we had no family history of twins, no extraordinary circumstances that would make twins more likely. Twins had never, ever been on the horizon. And yet there they were, plain as day on the ultrasound screen. That moment marked the dawning of my realization that parenthood is a journey filled with so many twists and turns that it is impossible to see what lies ahead.

Like many first-borns, I have always been something of a perfectionist. I found the prospect of being a perfect parent to a toddler and twin infants more than a bit daunting. In truth, I became so riddled with anxiety that I began preparing for the twins' arrival much as a king would ready his castle for a long and difficult siege. I immediately began making plans which involved all sorts of changes. My son's calm, rhythmic little world was descending into chaos.

We traded the sedan for a minivan and hired a contractor to add a second story to our home. As my belly expanded, so did my preoccupation and worry, deeply impacting my sensitive boy. I remember him sobbing as we said our goodbyes to his beloved gray car. The echoes of his lispy words, "Tell Mr. Gary to put my roof back on!" are also etched in my memory. Change after change took place, and as diligently as I tried to prepare him for it, I secretly feared that the birth of the twins would be Thomas's undoing.

The twins' arrival heralded even more change. We stayed at my parents' house for ten weeks while ours was under construction. Thomas outgrew his crib and moved to a toddler bed. Myriads of visitors paraded in and out, inevitably making more of a fuss over the adorable infants than their big brother. All four of us adults were exhausted and doing our best just to keep our heads above water. Although each of us made it a priority to spend time with him, Thomas clearly felt lost in the shuffle. The proof was in the pictures: in the dozens of photos taken during that time, there is not one in which Thomas is smiling.

At long last, we moved home, and each day my saint of a mother came to help, arriving early in the morning and staying until after dinner time. Thanks to her, I hung on to my sanity – but the toll became too steep. One morning, during an outing with Thomas, my mother began experiencing chest pain. In a swirly haze of panic myself, I tried to calm Thomas as I departed with my mother in the ambulance and neighbors rushed over to care for the kids. Many hours later, I returned home with a mixed bag of news. The good news: it wasn't a heart attack. The bad news: my mother's activities were to be sharply curtailed for the next several months. "Nan," as we lovingly call my mom, was to spend no more than three hours a day at our house. Thomas missed his beloved Nan sorely, and was not happy to exchange her Mary Poppins' like demeanor for my often-unwashed, grumpy, overwhelmed presence.

But the trials were not over yet. Less than a month later, one day before my birthday, my father was rushed to the hospital with acute appendicitis. I'll never forget that snowy, anxious afternoon waiting for news. When it finally came, it was far worse than I had expected. My father's appendix had ruptured, he was septic, on a ventilator, and suffering seizures. One complication after another arose, and for many days my father hovered precariously between this world and the next.

I tried my best to care for Thomas and the girls, support my mother, and be with my dad. But the anxiety was palpable, and despite my calm exterior, Thomas was not fooled. He knew I was inches away from being right over the edge. He felt it. And then he reflected it back in the only way he knew how: with copious, tremendous tantrums. My poor little son, soaking up all that emotion, was trying to discharge it as best he could.

Finally, a few days before Christmas, weak, and still quite ill, my father returned home. We saw my mother briefly Christmas morning, but it wasn't much of a holiday. All of us were too emotionally wrung out to really celebrate.

A week later, as we rung in the New Year, and prepared to celebrate Thomas's third birthday, Ted and I hoped that the worst was behind us. But the perfect storm that had become our lives had one more blow to deliver: Ted lost his job and was unable to find work in his field of expertise. My husband was devastated, money was tight, both of us were tense once again. As weeks of unemployment stretched into months, our anxiety grew – and so did Thomas's reaction to it.

3 THE EXPLOSIVE CHILD

By age three, Thomas had morphed from a gentle, joyful little boy into an angry, explosive child. He was on edge all the time, and it took almost nothing to send him into an all-out rage. His violence was frightening: ripping pieces of trim from the doorways, punching holes in the walls, breaking one thing after another. While one part of me ached for Thomas, another part was angry and resentful. Wasn't I busy enough without having to deal with an out-of-control child on top of everything else? Didn't he see how hard I was trying? Instead of turning to me for comfort, Thomas made me the constant focus of his rage. What had happened to our beautiful love affair? Unbelievably, it felt like we had become bitter enemies.

Around this time, Thomas also decided he was no longer going to be a boy. Boys, he announced, were stupid and boring. He cast off his male clothing, and chose the most girlish items he could find: princess dresses, mermaid costumes - the pinker and frillier, the better. He donned a hooded baby towel which became his long, flowing hair. Except for shampooing, we literally didn't see his head for over a year. This caused all of us adults quite a lot of anxiety. My instinct told me that this switch was directly tied to all of the attention his sisters received. But I hadn't yet learned to trust my instincts, and so began researching what experts had to say about this phenomenon.

From experts, I learned that while trying out the opposite gender was typical of children his age, the persistence with which Thomas denied his true gender was worrisome. I was informed that mermaid costumes were particularly ominous, sometimes revealing a child who was transgendered. Foolishly, I then watched a documentary about transgendered children which pushed me nearly into despair. I remember curling up next to my darling boy's warm, sleeping little form (still clad in his towel hair), sobbing, as I tried to summon up the courage it would take to allow him to become the girl he was perhaps meant to be.

In the midst of all this, it came time to register for preschool. Although I had already decided that we would homeschool, I felt an obligation to send

Thomas to preschool for the socialization. Experts emphasized how key this early social experience was for future success (success for what, I never really questioned. But I suspect they meant that it helped kids be more ready to accept the unnatural limits and expectations that would be foisted upon them come kindergarten). I was still very much a perfectionistic, rule-oriented parent at that point. I prided myself on knowing all the latest research and always doing the absolute best thing for my child. Besides, my mother had been a preschool director for years, and the program at her school sounded low-key and play-based. It seemed like a good fit.

As the school suggested, I registered Thomas for preschool a full 11 months ahead of time, and hoped that by the time Thomas actually arrived for his first day our stormy times would have finally given way to a clear horizon. But that September, as Thomas entered preschool, cloudy weather still prevailed. Knowing Thomas reserved his worst for at home, I was cautiously optimistic. Maybe he'd be okay at school. Maybe having his own special thing to do would be good for him. I crossed my fingers, offered up many a prayer, and hoped for the best.

4 WELCOME TO PRESCHOOL

For the first couple of weeks of preschool, it was smooth sailing. Thomas separated easily and seemed to have a good time at school. But that promising beginning quickly proved to be nothing but a short-lived honeymoon period. It became more and more difficult to get Thomas ready for school each morning, as he protested and did what he could to delay the inevitable. I'll never forget the infamous "battle of the pajamas."

"Thomas, let's look at your chart," I sang out that morning. It was a cute little chart I'd made myself, with pictures representing eating breakfast, brushing teeth and getting dressed. A smiley face could be velcroed underneath each picture to show where Thomas was in the process. This particular morning, the smiley face was depressingly stuck, refusing to leave the tooth brush icon in favor of the one showing an outfit.

"Oh, dear," I lamented, "I see the smiley face still isn't ready to move to getting dressed. We have just five more minutes before we have to leave for school."

"I'm not dressed because I'm not going!" Thomas stomped loudly down the hall, leaving me no choice but to follow. I was getting annoyed, but was determined not to let it show.

Calm and impartial, I replied, "Well, it is a school day, and school is your job, so you will be going. You can choose to go in your clothes, like a big boy, or I can take you in your pajamas."

"I'm not getting dressed!" Thomas shouted, and sat down angrily on the floor.

Armed with my knowledge of choices and natural consequences, I calmly packed an outfit in his backpack and packed Thomas and his sisters into the car. I was sure he'd break down and change once we got there. No dice. Thomas stuck to his guns. As our car inched forward in the drop off line, I found myself growing more and more agitated. When our turn finally came, Thomas was still in his light blue puppy pajamas. I was a wreck, trying to do a good impression of a calm and confident parent who was totally fine with the natural consequence of her kid showing up in nightwear.

"Good morning, Miss Michelle," I began, cool as a cucumber – externally, anyway. "As you can see, Thomas has chosen not to wear his clothes today. Although we've talked about how children wear clothes to school, he is not willing to get dressed. I've packed him an outfit in case he changes his mind."

Thomas not so calmly explained that he was wearing pajamas because he was not going to school. Miss Michelle scooped him up, gave him a hug and assured him he'd have a great day no matter what he was wearing. My last glimpse of his tiny pajama-clad figure heading through the heavy, black door was my undoing. I wept all the way home.

At the time, I was certain I was doing the right thing. I was following the advice of all the parenting experts and that of my friends who had walked this path before me. Be clear with your expectations, they informed me. Present the choices without emotion, and let your child experience the consequences. You're doing it for his own good! Children need to learn to separate. You do your part, let the teachers do theirs, and eventually he'll straighten out.

Day after day, my son told me he didn't want to go to school. He told me with his words. He told me with his behavior. And, earnestly desiring to do right by him, I turned a deaf ear.

5 WHEN IN DOUBT, TEST

I'm amazed now at how I turned something so straightforward into something so complicated. Thomas would tell me he didn't like school. I'd point out all of the great things about school. He'd tell me he wanted to be home with me. I'd explain why it was important that he leave me. Somewhere inside me there was a deep, unexamined belief that I would not be a good mother if I didn't insist that Thomas experience preschool. Good parents didn't give up, or give in. They supported and advocated. That, I knew how to do. I'd worked in special education for years. I requested a conference and got the ball rolling.

On the day of the conference, I was ushered to an unused room upstairs where I found myself being greeted by a host of teachers. I'd expected one, maybe two at most. But as I made my way across the bright red carpet to take my seat at the foot of a large, oblong conference table, I counted five teachers as well as the preschool director.

As a special educator, I was no stranger to parent-teacher conferences or team meetings. But never before had I realized how intimidating it could feel to be one parent among so many professionals. Never mind that we were ostensibly all here to work as a team. On the most basic of levels, in the simplest of terms, we were on opposite sides. Parent. Teacher. School. Home. And my side seemed woefully underrepresented.

We quickly got down to business, each teacher sharing her observations. It took a Herculean effort to listen to each one in turn, trying to be impartial, trying to listen attentively and nod my head at all the right places while inwardly, I struggled to maintain my composure.

As the last teacher spoke her piece I discovered I was in for even more disturbing news. While most of the teachers at Thomas's preschool were deeply committed to supporting children, working with parents and finding ways to make school a successful, happy place, Thomas's lead teacher felt strongly that Thomas's "problems" were mainly the result of a poor upbringing. And she made no secret of it.

"Maybe this is a boy who has just too many choices at home," she suggested, in a tone that implied there was no "maybe" about it.

Astonished, I found myself looking around the table at the others, searching for some indication of whether they agreed. Suddenly I felt very much like a defendant taking the stand. What could I say that would convince these people that I was a good mother? That Thomas's problems weren't all my fault?

I protested that I carefully followed the exact parenting program the preschool promoted. Two choices at most: this or that, and once the choice was made, we stuck to it. Logical and natural consequences ensued. They'd already seen it in action; need I remind them of the unforgettable "pajama day"?

When her 'overly permissive' theory didn't hold water, Miss Marlene critiqued my delivery of said parenting program. "We notice he looks at our faces for too long after we've said something to him," Miss Marlene proffered, "Like he can't read our emotion. It's quite possible that you're not using enough emotion in your face and voice, and he's now become stunted – unable to determine people's emotions - and he acts out due to this frustration."

I felt myself growing uncomfortably hot. What was Miss Marlene talking about? In all my years as a special educator I'd never heard a suggestion quite as ludicrous as this one. Granted, I usually had a fairly calm exterior, especially out in public.

But *come on!* I was raising a challenging toddler and twin babies. Did she seriously think I possessed the emotional wherewithal to keep emotion out my parenting? Most days I could barely think straight. Calm, cool and collected was definitely not the norm at that point. I told her so - not quite so calmly. I was horrified to feel my eyes threatening to fill with tears. I fought for control. I would *not* let this woman see me cry. On some level, I feared such a sign of weakness would only add fuel to her fire.

Other teachers sprinkled in questions here and there, but I was too shaken to answer thoroughly. My mind felt like it was working in slow motion. I couldn't seem to digest the information they offered or formulate thoughtful responses. Sweat trickled down my back, soaking my shirt and pooling at my waistband. I hoped no one would notice.

When it became evident that attacking my parenting skills was not going over well, Miss Marlene changed her tactics. "Well, if it's nothing you're doing at home, then it looks like we may have a very troubled little boy on our hands. I suggest you have a full core evaluation done on him right away." She loaded me up with names and contact numbers, urging me to get right on this because the process could take a while. In the interim, she strongly suggested that we try taking a very firm line with any and all misbehavior: showing more anger at Thomas's transgressions and implementing more severe consequences.

Miss Marlene's recommendations made it obvious what she was thinking: either we were failures as parents, or Thomas was inherently flawed. Either way, the news was devastating.

6 ENTER THE SPECIAL EDUCATION MOTHER

I spent the next several weeks inwardly grieving. I tried to figure out where I'd gone wrong, how I'd failed in spite of trying so hard. *Was* it my parenting, as Miss Marlene had suggested? Had my diet been somehow lacking during my pregnancy? Perhaps something had happened during Thomas's birth. Or maybe I should've waited until he was older to have another baby. Round and round I went, analyzing every action, every decision, every life event that could have signaled the first misstep.

Entrenched as I was in mainstream, conventional parenting, it never occurred to me to explore the simplest answer of all: Thomas wasn't ready to leave me. He'd been through more than a year of major changes: changes that had come fast and furious, and had rocked us to our core. He had been displaced by not one but two small intruders who seemed to command the attention of everyone in sight. He'd exchanged a set of stable, loving parents for a couple of sleep-deprived raving lunatics. Nothing was the same: not his home, not his family, and certainly not his circumstances.

The bond which had tied us so closely when Thomas was a baby had become badly frayed. In his three-year-old wisdom, Thomas knew the remedy. He needed to be with me. To reconnect. To reestablish the close, trusting relationship we'd once had. But I'd forfeited simple wisdom to expert advice and a world full of judgment. Let him quit? Keep him home? I could just hear the voices condemning me.

You can't just let him quit. He'll grow up thinking he can wimp out whenever the going gets tough!

What, does the kid run the show around here? You're the parent, you know what's best for him, and you've got to stick to your guns!

A child with behavior issues this severe needs to be diagnosed and serviced. What kind of parent just buries her head in the sand, hoping the problems will go away by themselves? You've got to do something!

The voices in my head were thunderous and incessant. They drowned out my inner wisdom. And they drowned out my son's.

Afraid to delay, let alone choose a different

course, I contacted the pupil services department of the local school and requested a full core evaluation. I met with my pediatrician and took down the names and numbers of several local neuropsychologists. But I didn't stop there. Thomas was failing in school. If he were going to end the year on a positive note, he would need support - more support than his teachers could give him. Luckily, I had the answer: I called the director of the preschool and asked that I be allowed to accompany Thomas to school as a one-to-one assistant until the end of the school year. I'd been a special educator. I knew what to do. I got right down to work.

I created a variety of social stories and scripts about school, which Thomas and I read daily. These were designed to help Thomas internalize ideas and behaviors. "School is a safe place for Thomas," read one script. "The boys and girls want to be friends." I wonder now how Thomas processed the great disconnect between what he was hearing and what he was actually experiencing. After all, saying it doesn't magically make it so. I may have believed my own carefully crafted words, but Thomas was too crafty to fall for it.

In order to minimize the difficulty of transitions, Thomas and I planned the school day with icons on a portable schedule. That way,

Thomas knew what to expect. Of course, it also meant the death of any spontaneity, but I figured that was a small price to pay.

Next, I introduced signal cards for breaks. If Thomas felt that he was becoming overwhelmed, he could present me with a signal card, and we would leave the activity and find someplace quiet in order to regroup. How strange this must have seemed to Thomas! At home, we spoke to each other like regular people. If he was sick of something, he said so. But at school, everything was different. We were no longer parent and child. We were student and teacher.

When Thomas's behavior was appropriate, I rewarded him. When it was inappropriate, I removed him. I was the quintessential special education teacher, managing his behaviors in accordance with my training.

In spite of my rather dubious underlying agenda, Thomas began to feel safer at school. And as a result, something pretty miraculous started to happen. Thomas began taking the initiative to regain his independence.

"Mommy," he whispered to me one morning after circle time, "I think I can play by myself at the craft table. You wait for me over by the guinea pig, and I'll call you if I need you."

You could have knocked me over with a feather.

But this was only the beginning. More and more, Thomas strayed from my side in order to play, explore, and interact with other children.

Miss Michelle was especially interested in the different methods I used to support Thomas. After a few weeks, she began shadowing us, preparing to be Thomas's "safe" person should the need arise. Soon, it did.

"Mommy, I think I'm ready to go to school without you some of the time," Thomas proudly announced one sunny spring day. "Can I try Fridays all by myself?" Delighted, I spoke with Miss Michelle, who agreed to take on my usual role every Friday.

That first Friday I dropped Thomas off by himself, I was a nervous wreck. I kept waiting for the phone to ring, delivering the news I dreaded: that Thomas hadn't been able to handle the challenge.

But it was a bouncy, smiling boy who proudly walked out to the car at pick up time. "Fantastic day!" Miss Michelle proclaimed, and gave me the details while Thomas happily climbed into his car seat. And so it was with every Friday after.

As I talked over this surprising turn of events with my husband and my mother, all three of us were struck by the depth of wisdom and self-knowledge Thomas possessed. Somewhere deep inside, he knew exactly how far he could comfortably stretch himself, and exactly what conditions he needed in order to do so successfully.

Meanwhile, things were moving forward with the school's evaluation. We met with a host of specialists: an occupational therapist, a school psychologist, a guidance counselor, a speech and language therapist, and a special education teacher. Thomas had several sessions with each. He seemed fairly willing to go off with these total strangers, despite the fact that I was relegated to a plastic couch in the corridor. There I sat, reading any and all research I could get my hands on while I awaited Thomas's return. Far be it from a *perfect* parent to spend that time any other way.

By late spring, the results were in, the reports were written, and the team meeting scheduled. Before the meeting, I scoured the reports, making notes, highlighting passages, marking down questions and comments. If this kid could be figured out and fixed through due diligence, then I was ready to bring my 'A' game.

I remember walking in to the team meeting thinking how surreal it all seemed. How many times had I sat on the opposite side of that table, delivering devastating news to some poor, vulnerable parent? How many times had I arrogantly assumed that because I held a degree, I knew what that child needed better than his or her own parents did? How could I have failed to overlook the years of experience those parents had brought to the table?

Well, I was the one in the parent seat now. Only, I knew something most parents don't know as they perch on their tiny plastic chairs, waiting for the verdict. I knew what that formidable team of experts was thinking. I knew their language. I knew their approach. And I had a pretty good idea of what they were saying to one another before I'd entered the room and after I'd exited. I thought this would be an advantage. It wasn't. Instead, it was the worst kind of torture.

In order to avoid a complete breakdown, I entered that meeting as a colleague rather than a parent. I donned my "special educator" hat and hid underneath. I spoke as professionally as possible. I tried to appear well-informed, open to ideas, and highly rational. And underneath it all, I hated every single person sitting so smugly in that meeting, thinking that after a few tests and a bit of observation they knew more about my son than I did.

I listened as each recited a monologue of Thomas's flaws and foibles pertaining to their area of specialty. They walked me through a string of tests and subtests, describing each one and summarizing Thomas's performance. I was struck by how confusing it was to be presented with so much information, to try to take it all in - and I had the advantage of having worked in the field! What must it be like, I wondered, for the parents who were hearing this for the first time?

Having already scrutinized the reports, none of what the specialists said was news, really. But that didn't make it any less upsetting - or embarrassing - to hear the words spoken aloud. I felt an acute sense of shame and judgment. I had an "atypical" child. Perhaps it was because I was a deficient parent. Perhaps it was because Thomas was genetically flawed. Either way, it was profoundly humiliating. Whether these people were peddling pity or judgment, I wanted no part of either.

In all fairness, some of the people at that table were lovely – kind, approachable, and clearly dedicated to finding ways to support my son. Some were markedly less so. But in the end, what rankled was that any of them thought that what their tests could tell me outranked what I knew in my flesh and bone. I knew my boy through and through. He was my heart, my world. To them, he was the 4.3 year old with a high IQ and some seriously weird testing results.

After the presentation, I was given a chance to ask questions. Having done my research, I offered my take on what the testing results indicated. I pointed to a large spread in certain testing values and mentioned fancy words such as "non-verbal learning disability" and "mild prosopagnosia". I sensed, rather than saw, the professionals exchanging knowing glances. *Here's one who just can't accept the facts*, I could almost hear them saying to one another, *How pathetic!*

In the true, "Give us your tired, give us your poor" spirit, the team graciously offered Thomas a slot in the integrated preschool for the fall. Not one of their "typical" slots, but as one of the "special needs" students. He would be put on an Individualized Education Plan (implying, by the way, that only "atypical" children deserve an individualized education). Thomas would receive free busing, free tuition, and the personal oversight of his liaison. Lucky, lucky us. Who knew all the perks that came along with having an officially troubled child?

In the meantime, they urged, we should have Thomas further evaluated. Although qualified to *test*, the team explained, they were not at liberty to *diagnose*. Little did I know that some of them were already leaning heavily toward a diagnosis, and were merely looking for confirmation. Little did I know how far off their conclusions would prove to be.

For an official diagnosis, we would need to see an expert. I was given a name and number and encouraged to make contact right away, as it could take months to actually get an appointment, and it was essential that a diagnosis be in place well before Thomas entered kindergarten.

I left that meeting with the most disconcerting feeling. Seeing myself through their eyes, I lost my true sense of self. Who was I? Who was I going to be in light of these developments? Was I the dedicated, loving mother I'd always believed myself to be? Was I that troublesome parent teachers couldn't stand - the one who just wouldn't get on board and accept what they recommended without question? Or was I the pitiful parent too much in denial, too deluded about her child's deficiencies to face up to reality?

Back at home, I related the latest developments to my mother, processing out loud as she lent a loving ear. *Take it one step at a time*, she advised. *You don't have to figure everything out right this minute.*

But the state of unrest and anxiety I experienced made it hard to take things slowly. Something was wrong with Thomas. *Okay then*, I decided, *let's figure this thing out and get him fixed.* Once again, I launched into action. I immediately scheduled the recommended appointment. I toured the integrated preschool, and set up a time for Thomas to visit his new classroom. At night, I pored over the reports and any resources I could find to shed additional light. If my child was going to be a special needs kid, I was determined that he would be the best special needs kid alive. And I'd be the best mother ever to set foot in that integrated preschool.

I became so focused on that label, "special needs", and on my perfection-driven response to it, that in the process I lost sight of my little boy. He was no longer a kid to cuddle, a person to appreciate, relate to, and connect with. He was my cause. And every time he didn't respond to my fabulous "special education parenting" I got frustrated. Not only was he not getting better, he was making me look bad. *Me*, the super special-educator turned perfect-parent who should be able to handle this with one hand tied behind my back. He should have been fixed in no time. So why on earth, I lamented, was he getting *worse*?

7 CHANGE IN PLANS

Thomas's fourth summer slowly wound down, and as it did, I could feel my anxiety gearing up. I was terribly conflicted about sending Thomas to the integrated preschool. On the one hand, I hoped that with all of the support he'd be receiving, he'd begin to make good progress. On the other hand, turning him over to people I barely knew left me weak in the knees. Most shameful of all to my mind: a part of me was secretly looking forward to our time apart. Life at home had become so unpredictable and tense, I found myself eager for the break.

Late in August, I received a call from Mrs. Abrams, the preschool special education teacher who had been a part of Thomas's core evaluation. Thomas had connected with Mrs. Abrams immediately, and had visited her class back in June when the decision had been made to place him in Mrs. Abrams class come September. Mrs. Abrams was calm and easy-going, and she seemed to "get" Thomas right from the get-go. Knowing he'd be spending his days with her was a comfort - a comfort that was about to be ripped away.

"Good morning, Mrs. Olson," Mrs. Abrams greeted me, "I hope you and Thomas have been enjoying your summer." I replied that we had, and inquired about hers. After a few minutes of chit-chat, Mrs. Abrams got to the point: "Mrs. Olson, I'm calling to let you know that I will not be Thomas's preschool teacher after all. Unfortunately, we're under-enrolled, and the decision has been made to dissolve my class."

I was stunned. The images I'd had about the upcoming school year had featured Mrs. Abrams front and center, lovingly caring for my boy in my absence. But in the numbers-driven world of public school, what mattered was how effectively the money was spent, not how much my son or I liked a certain teacher.

Mrs. Abrams told me a bit about Thomas's new teacher, Mrs. Lambsworth. She was a veteran teacher, Mrs. Abrams explained, and I could rest assured that she knew what she was doing. After wishing us a terrific school year, Mrs. Abrams bid me farewell and hung up.

Playing in the sunny backyard that afternoon, I remember feeling strangely chilled. Once again, my world - and Thomas's - was filled with uncertainty. Who was this woman I was entrusting with my son? Would she love him, be kind to him, keep him safe both physically and emotionally? Certainly she would, I persuaded myself.

But as it turned out, she would not.

8 THE BOY WITH THE NEMO BACKPACK

Two days before school began, Mrs. Lambsworth invited me in for a "get to know you" conference. She suggested I bring Thomas as well, so the two of them could meet. I left the twins with my mother, and Thomas and I headed off into the unknown.

We arrived at school and checked into the office. Thomas checked out the tropical fish residing in a large tank while I read through the visitors' instruction sheet, signed the visitors' log, and picked up two visitors' badges. It seemed strange to have to jump through so many hoops to be admitted into a school that years before I'd been required to attend. Not to mention that the school secretary and a host of other people already knew me. Such is life in a small town.

But in the slightly shabby, air-conditioned space of this office, relationships were beside the point. There was a protocol to be followed. Only after I was "officially" processed could the secretary and I chat about how big her kids had grown, how much they had loved my mother's preschool, and how she couldn't get over the family resemblance she saw in my adorable little guy.

After a bit, Mrs. Lambsworth made her way down the hall to retrieve us. As introductions were made, I was struck by the glaring differences between Mrs. Abrams and this new teacher. Mrs. Abrams was tall, vibrant, and had - in Thomas's words - a very smiley face. Mrs. Lambsworth was short, stocky, and serious. In all the months to follow, I never once saw her smile.

Still, we had no choice but to forge ahead - or so I thought - and so we followed her down to the classroom to get acquainted. Thomas wandered about the classroom, exploring, while Mrs. Lambsworth and I touched base. She was a hard worker, dedicated to her profession; that much was obvious. She'd spent much of her summer preparing her classroom for the beginning of school, she informed me, lugging furniture and boxes in the heat that was intensified by huge windows opposite the entrance. Since the windows only opened a crack, rather than admit any breeze, they seemed instead to act as a huge magnifying glass, focusing and concentrating the sun as it passed through. I was vaguely reminded of the unfortunate ants of my childhood.

Although Mrs. Lambsworth seemed pleasant, she didn't appear to connect with Thomas the way Mrs. Abrams had. I left the meeting hoping, rather than expecting, that she would be a good match for Thomas. Still, I tried to put on a brave face. As we drove home, I gushed about the classroom with great enthusiasm, pointing out the eye-catching decorations, the various learning centers, and the cubby already labeled with Thomas's name.

But Thomas wasn't buying what I was trying to sell. This was not what he was expecting, and he was not at all sure there were any redeeming qualities about the classroom - or his new teacher - whatsoever. While I bubbled on about the dress-up corner and the puzzle table, he persistently stuck to a single theme: this new lady may be many things, but she was most definitely *not* Mrs. Abrams. And Mrs. Abrams was who he'd signed up for.

Tragically, I was still steeped in the mainstream belief that adults always know better than children. No, Mrs. Lambsworth wasn't at all like Mrs. Abrams, and yes, it was a disappointing change, but the show must go on. We all agreed. There were problems to fix, special needs to address, and the right and proper place for that to occur was at the integrated preschool. I was completely stuck in the conventional philosophy: out of the box thinking was out of the question. Sure, I wasn't afraid to renovate an inside wall here or there, but the box remained firmly in place. I never questioned it. In fact, I'm not even sure I realized there *was* a box back in those days.

And so, despite my trepidation, when the first day of school finally rolled around, I made sure Thomas was dressed, packed, and ready to go when the tiny preschool bus rolled to a stop in front of our shady front porch. Squelching my misgivings, I confidently squeezed Thomas's hand as I led him to the bus where the aide was waiting at the top of the steps.

"Wow, Thomas, look at this bus!" I exclaimed brightly, "You're going to have such a fun ride to school!" With that, I began gently moving him up the stairs. After all, we didn't want to keep anybody waiting. Thomas resisted at first, his little body going stiff, slowly becoming diagonal as he feet ascended while the rest of him hung back. Luckily, the bus aide had the magic touch. She won him over with a quick wink and a, "Come wave out the window with me, Thomas!"

Thomas looked back at me for one brief moment, then, perhaps sensing the futility of further protest, righted himself and trudged up the stairs, offering Miss Deb a wan smile as he plopped down beside her. She helped Thomas buckle up as the doors swung shut, and he watched out the window as the bus began to pull away.

He looked so small, so defenseless in those final moments. His little legs had seemed so tiny as they stretched to climb each step, and his plump hand impossibly little as it reluctantly released mine. My gaze fell on Thomas's vibrant blue and orange Finding Nemo backpack propped beside him on the seat. It seemed far too festive for such uncertain times.

I waved and blew kisses. Thomas didn't wave back as he watched me with somber eyes - eyes that spoke of a sense of betrayal and terrible heartache.

The bus turned the corner and rolled out of sight. I stayed on the lawn watching anyway, as if my gaze could travel along beside Thomas all the way to school if only I concentrated deeply enough. I stood there, motionless, for long moments. Then I silently offered up yet another prayer, turned, and started for the door.

9 HOMECOMING

Three hours later, I restlessly haunted my front hallway, listening for signs of the bus that would deposit Thomas safely at home. I'd spent the interim attempting to enjoy some special time with the twins, but I was too distracted to make a convincing effort. Eventually, I'd put them down for a nap and then wandered around aimlessly, trying to be productive, but not quite knowing how to begin.

At long last, I heard the rumble of the bus as it turned the corner and came down the road toward our house. It stopped two doors down to deposit another little boy at my neighbor's daycare. The wait seemed eternal. Finally, the doors closed, the engine roared back to life, and the bus completed the final leg of its journey.

I zipped outside, armed with an absurdly bright smile and an enthusiastic greeting. "Hi, darling!" I chirped, "How was your first day of school? Did you have a terrific time?"

Thomas trudged down the stairs and past me. The bus driver assured me that he'd done very well on both rides, and that he'd had a good first day. After thanking the driver and the aide, I turned and hurried to catch up with Thomas as he opened the front door. He stepped inside, dropped his backpack, and immediately knocked his two-year old sister flat on her back. "Dumb sissy!" he yelled.

As I scooped up Faith to console her, Thomas marched over to Katy and began poking her tummy - hard. "Mush!" he yelled, "Mush! Mush! Mush!"

Within seconds Katy was crying, too. What had just happened? I quickly put Faith down and whisked Katy up and away from the inexplicable assault. Without a word, Thomas turned and knocked Faith over again.

"STOP!" I bellowed, but he wouldn't - maybe he couldn't. I put Katy down and this time went straight for the source. I lifted Thomas up and headed for the time-out spot. Thomas hit me repeatedly as I carried him over to the time-out rug and plunked him down. Then he proceeded to scream at the top of his lungs. He grabbed a boot that was within arm's reach and flung it at Katy's head. As I scrambled to move everything out of his reach, Thomas began kicking the wall. Ugly black scuffs scarred the light green paint. The screaming was ear-splitting.

The twins, frightened and hurt, joined in the cacophony. I was paralyzed. In the space of two minutes, Thomas's tirade had completely destroyed the peace of everyone in the house. I looked back and forth, from the crying twins to the raging Thomas, helpless to soothe any of them. I knew if I turned to comfort one of the girls, Thomas would be on top of the other faster than lightning. The best I could do was to stand guard and wait for the storm to subside.

Welcome home, I thought angrily, *it sure is great to have you back.* I glared at Thomas resentfully. What was *wrong* with him? It seemed the more support he got, the more angry and violent he became. And it was a struggle not to blame him for it.

****

Looking back at that disastrous first day, how I wish the more seasoned mother I am now could have whispered wisdom to the desperate mother I was back then. "Breathe," I would have counseled, "Find your own stillness and center. No need to panic. Take a step back and see what is truly going on here."

I'd like to think that long-ago mother would have

been able to gain a new perspective in those moments. I'd like to think that it all would have become clear. She'd have taken a deep breath, and known in an instant exactly what she needed to do. Trusting that the girls would be all right for a few minutes, she would have turned to her anguished little boy. She would have sat down in front of him on that time-out rug and radiated her love and acceptance.

"Thomas, sweetie, you're so upset," she would begin, "I'm right here. I'm going to help you. Come, sit in my lap until you're feeling safe and sound."

Her words and her energy would soothe him. Slowly the tension would drain from his body. He'd curl up in her lap. After a while, he'd begin to open up, telling her about his difficult day. She would rock him as she listened. And she would truly hear.

If only I'd had the knowledge and the confidence back then to follow my instincts, perhaps everything would have been different. Perhaps we would have been able to start the healing process so much sooner.

Perhaps I would not be writing this story.

10 TROUBLE WITH MAISIE

The first few weeks of school slipped by. I didn't hear much from Thomas's teachers, and I heard even less from Thomas himself. I told myself that no news was good news, and that I didn't want to be one of *those* parents - the over-anxious helicopter type who constantly pestered an already harried teacher. On the other hand, I certainly didn't want to seem uninterested. My angst was surely palpable.

And then, with all the sudden unexpectedness of self-fulfilling prophesies, the phone call I'd been half-listening for finally arrived.

"Mrs. Olson, Mrs. Lambsworth here. We're having some problems with Thomas, and we need to talk. He's been assaulting a little girl, and her father's quite upset about it."

I was unsurprised and flabbergasted simultaneously.

Here at home, Thomas had become increasingly angry and violent. School days were the worst. Thomas attended the afternoon sessions, and as the morning wore on, he became more and more irritable. Usually, I managed to get him out the door and onto the bus without a major blowup, but it was always touch and go. I'm sure Thomas sensed the anxiety I felt about the possibility of a meltdown, and it only fueled the fire.

Afternoons were horrible. Thomas came home on the attack. I had to put systems in place just to keep the girls safe from bodily harm. I'd set them up in the playroom, zip out and get Thomas off the bus, usher him inside and walk him directly upstairs to his room. After a while, he'd wander down, usually calm enough for me to head off any attacks - if I paid close attention to the warning signs.

And so, when the call came, it wasn't all that surprising. But it *was* horrifying. I was beyond embarrassed to have my child be *that* kid - the one that all the other parents despise. The one that everyone hopes won't be in their child's class the next year. And I couldn't bear to think of the way this little girl's father must be judging me. He must think Thomas came from a troubled or neglectful home. Perhaps he envisioned me as a slovenly, ignorant shrew who had no clue as to how to raise her kid. Maybe he thought there was alcohol or drug abuse. At the very least, he had to believe that I was shirking my parental duties, because no kid with responsible parents would be repeatedly attacking a classmate.

I listened as Mrs. Lambsworth described the nature of the attacks. It seemed that Thomas was picking this little girl up around the middle and squeezing her. Sometimes he poked her stomach. Once in a while, he'd attempt to stroke her hair, sometimes pulling it when she tried to get away.

"So, Mrs. Olson, as you can see, we have a major problem here. Do you have any thoughts?"

"Thoughts? About why he's doing that, you mean?" I inquired, a bit unsure of what she was asking.

"Well, yes, I suppose - but mainly I'm wondering how you think we should handle it," Mrs. Lambsworth responded.

A jumble of thoughts whirled through my brain. Why was *she* asking *me* how to handle it? Wasn't she the professional? And wasn't there an entire team of specialists meeting monthly to discuss Thomas's progress and brainstorm strategies? Was this a courtesy, a mark of respect for a former colleague? Or was it more of a "let's handle this one with kid gloves or she could make our lives a nightmare" kind of move?

I didn't know. I couldn't think. My mind went numb, threatening to shut down completely. Just in the nick of time, I remembered my special ed teacher hat. I pulled it out and dove headlong underneath.

"Mrs. Lambsworth, thank you so much for bringing this to my attention," I replied calmly. "Rest assured that I will speak to Thomas about it. In the meantime, I will be happy to come up with a list of possible actions to take. May I send it in Thomas's backpack tomorrow?"

Mrs. Lambsworth assented, and after agreeing to speak in a few days' time, we hung up. Instantly, my brain was flooded with thoughts, none clear enough to examine. I began absently unloading the dishwasher full of dirty dishes. Halfway through, I realized my blunder. As I searched through drawers for still-soiled silverware, Thomas came barreling in, demanding a snack.

"I'm busy!" I snapped. "And by the way, why are you attacking that little girl in your class? Mrs. Lambsworth says her father is furious about it."

All of my pent up emotion spilled out, landing squarely on my four-year-old's shoulders. He looked up at me, staring far too long. *Not reading my emotion?* I thought, bitterly. *It ought to be pretty easy: I'm humiliated - and it's your fault.*

After several moments, Thomas shifted his gaze. His eyes grew hard, his face impassive. He whirled around and stomped out of the kitchen, but not before swiping an old cup of juice off the counter and all over the floor.

That evening, as I tucked Thomas into bed, he told me he was too frightened to go to sleep.

I tucked an errant strand of hair behind his ears. "Why, honey? What are you scared of?"

"I'm scared Maisie's daddy will come in my room and punch me 'cuz he's so mad about what I did to Maisie. Mommy, do you think he can get inside our house? *Did you lock the doors?*" Thomas's eyes were wide with fear.

I tried to find the perfect balance between reassuring him that he was safe, and keeping him just worried enough to motivate him to leave Maisie alone.

"Maisie's dad is not going to come here and hurt you," I told Thomas. "But if you keep bothering Maisie, he might ask for a conference. He might want to speak to you. And he might be pretty angry at you."

****

"Stop," today's mother pleads, "don't you realize what you're doing? You're siding against your son. In his eyes, you've just shoved him right under the bus, turned your back, and walked away. He's a tiny child. He doesn't understand all of his behaviors, or the powerful emotions that shape them. He needs you to be

there for him. To see his own best self, to help him sort through the scary, confusing feelings. He's longing for you to love him unconditionally and to protect him from angry fathers and reproving teachers. Don't let your fear of failure and your worries about what others might think keep you from giving your beloved child what he needs most."

****

But I couldn't hear that voice back then. The judgment, the self-doubt, and the words of the experts left no space of silence, no moment when that instinctual mother-wisdom might have had a chance to shine through.

As it happened, the following week Thomas had a field trip to which we parents were invited. As we gathered in the classroom waiting for the loudspeaker to summon us to the bus, I caught my first glimpse of Maisie. She was tiny, looking more like two than four. Her long, strawberry blonde hair was swept up in a perky ponytail. She looked remarkably familiar. And when I realized why, everything suddenly fell into place.

11 PUZZLE PIECES

Crouching down beside Thomas, I subtly gestured to the tiny girl over by the chalkboard. "Hey, buddy, that's Maisie, isn't it?"

"Maisie!" Thomas yelled, pointing. His face took on an odd look, eyes wide, a too-big smile pasted on his mouth. He laughed a monotone laugh, repeating himself even more loudly, "Maisie, Maisie, Maisie!"

I hated when he did this. It made him look so different - so weird. It was as if my sweet son had fled the premises and left in his place an unusually large toddler.

Maisie's father raised his head and scanned the room, looking for the source of the commotion. Quickly, I shielded Thomas from his gaze, lowered his stiff, pointing arm and instructed him to hush in an angry, whispered tone of my own.

Soon we were shepherded onto the bus, and

began a long, slow ride to the farm. Thomas's body angled away from me, looking out the window. I tried to engage him in conversation, but stopped after a few failed attempts. Instead, I thought over the puzzle that seemed to be falling into place...

By the time the twins were about one, Thomas had developed a strong preference for one over the other. Katy became his darling little sister, while he absolutely despised Faith. It was as if he took those conflicting internal feelings all siblings have for one another, and divided them right down the middle. All the jealousy and anger became focused on Faith. All the feelings of love and loyalty he showered upon Katy.

Over time, Thomas seemed to focus more and more on Katy, especially when he was anxious or upset. He loved her pudgy little tummy, and would poke it - not always gently - when he needed to soothe himself. As he grew stronger, and she grew sturdier, he loved to come up behind her and pick her up around the waist, squeezing her tight like a beloved stuffed animal. He was fascinated by her silky, smooth strawberry blond hair, and loved to run his fingers through it. Somehow, Katy had become more than Thomas's favorite sister. She had become his security blanket as well.

As Thomas's life grew increasingly turbulent,

his relationship with Katy and Faith became more and more polarized. He tormented Faith relentlessly. His constant attempts to find comfort with Katy left her feeling crowded and defensive. Both sisters grew fearful of him, and began to pull back from his boisterous, unpredictable presence. I can only imagine how this new source of rejection and pain must have impacted my sensitive son.

All of this swirled through my mind as I gazed absently at Maisie, sitting three rows ahead of us. She looked remarkably like my daughter Katy, from her size to her hair color. Were Thomas's "attacks" actually attempts to calm himself at school, similar to his interactions with Katy at home?

That night, after bedtime stories and prayers, I brought up the subject of Maisie again. "So, Maisie seems like a pretty nice little girl," I remarked.

"I LOVE her!" Thomas threw open his arms to drive home his words.

"What do you love about her?"

"She's so mushy and cute!" This, incidentally, was exactly how Thomas described Katy. My theory seemed to be correct.

"So how come you grab her and pull her hair?"

Thomas's eyes bore into mine as he protested, "I don't do that! I love her! I love to mush her and feel her ponytail. But Mrs. Lambsworth always takes me away and makes me sit on the calm-down rug."

We talked for a bit longer, Thomas professing his love for Maisie, while I tried to explain how his behavior might feel to her. We came up with some alternatives he could try instead of squeezing her or touching her hair.

The next day, I called Mrs. Lambsworth and gave her my take on the situation. She listened politely, but seemed unconvinced. I suggested writing a social story - a short, personalized story to address Thomas's interactions with Maisie - and using some of his therapy time to practice the alternatives I'd suggested. Mrs. Lambsworth gave me a non-committal reply.

Next, I asked her if Thomas seemed unhappy or anxious while at school, since those were the times I saw his "Katy" behaviors at home. No, he didn't seem unhappy, Mrs. Lambsworth replied. But he was very uncooperative, only interested in doing what he wanted to do. When it came to therapy or group skill time, he was quite hard to manage. He'd get really silly, or become oppositional, simply refusing to do the task. But anxious? No, he didn't seem anxious at all.

****

The trained professional in me considered Mrs. Lambsworth's observations in light of special education practice. My focus was on how to change Thomas's behaviors - how to get him to perform the required tasks. The answer was simple: modify the task, have an aide sit next to him to keep him focused, and put a reward system into place to encourage him to comply. Not once did I question that it may be the school's basic premise that was the problem, and not my son's reaction to it.

If only I'd been able to hear my mother-wisdom interject: "Why is everyone so focused on getting him to comply? Have you tried asking him why he doesn't want to? Have you tried to discover what he wants to do instead? After all, this is preschool. It's supposed to be fun!

If only I'd understood that my son, in his child-like wisdom, was communicating a profound truth. Sure, his words sounded simplistic. "I don't want to do that." But underneath those words there was an unarticulated yet fully formed belief: that he should be able to direct his time as he saw fit. That he should be engaging in that which was inspiring and enjoyable. And that belief begged a question: When an individual is being coerced to do something that is neither interesting nor seen to be of value to that individual, is refusing to comply truly a maladaptive response? Or is it actually the most natural response of all?

12 THE CENTER

After my conversation with Mrs. Lambsworth, I began talking more with Thomas about school - or at least, I tried to. Getting Thomas to open up was like pulling teeth. He'd reply to my questions with one word responses - if at all. Most often, he'd simply change the subject. If I pressed him, Thomas would either get silly or belligerent. In any case, we never got very far.

This was especially frustrating since I really wanted his take on things. I was beginning to hear more and more from Thomas's teacher and special education liaison that he was not progressing as expected. His behavior was deteriorating, requiring an inordinate amount of time from the aides in the room.

"This can't continue," I was informed, "after all, his IEP doesn't call for a one-to-one. It's simply not fair to the other children if he monopolizes so much of the adults' time." Each conversation ended with a reference to the upcoming diagnostic appointment. Could I get it moved up? Maybe get on a cancellation list? Getting a diagnosis was crucial, they reminded me, if they were going to be able to service Thomas effectively.

I came away from each of these conversations with a vague sense that something was very wrong. First of all, nobody there seemed to like my little boy very much. Instead, they seemed annoyed that he was such a behavior problem. This didn't gel with my own experience as a special educator.

Where I had taught, we really loved each child - even the tough ones. Sometimes *especially* the tough ones. And when one of my students with special needs was struggling, I neither blamed the child nor his parents. If anything, I blamed myself for not finding a way to help that student be successful. The entire team worked together, continually striving to find better ways to support the children in our charge.

Again, I was torn. My instinct told me one thing. My training told me another. It seemed so unlikely that the professionals may not be handling things correctly. And all this judgment I was feeling? Surely it had to be a misperception. And yet, I couldn't shake the feeling that the experts thought the problem was, at its root, something entirely different from what I believed it to be.

Following Mrs. Lambsworth's advice, I phoned the center at which we'd scheduled Thomas's evaluation and explained the situation. Unfortunately, it wasn't possible to get an earlier appointment. We were looking at six months out, at best. They did, however, have an opening with an occupational therapist, who could at least perform that part of the evaluation and recommend services. She was available the following week. I marked it down on my calendar.

One week later, Thomas and I traveled forty-five minutes to meet with the OT. After an unusually difficult time finding parking, we finally arrived at the office, and stepped into the waiting area.

It was a brightly decorated, kid-friendly area, and Thomas was immediately drawn to the train table set in the middle. I checked in, then took a seat near Thomas and began filling out the paperwork. Just then, a loud, guttural sound to my left startled me, and my pen swerved messily below the line. As I looked up, a large boy of about twelve leaped out of his seat and ran toward the train table. The other children shrank back. The boy's father was close behind. Quickly, he took the boy's arm and led him back to the chairs.

"Sit-time," he instructed. He firmly pushed down on the boy's shoulders until his knees began to bend. Slowly the boy sank into his seat.

The boy leaned his head into his father's side, pleading "rub, rub?" over and over. The dad's palm made circles on the top of the boy's head. Eventually, the boy became quiet.

Thomas had been startled by the boy, too. I saw him watching the boy the way one watches a bee in the room: intently, and with readiness to flee should the danger come too close.

As I looked around, I saw child after child with atypical behaviors. One was rocking back and forth while looking at a spinning toy. Another kept pulling her own hair every time her mother let go of her hands. A third child paced up and down, his hands flapping strangely by his sides. Every so often, he stopped, raised his hands and clapped his ears twice. The pacing then resumed.

Just exactly what kind of center was this? I wondered. The cutesy name was optimistic but completely vague. I scanned the registration papers more closely. In small print, under the center's adorable logo, were the words, "specializing in autism and other brain dysfunction". Thomas's teachers wanted a diagnosis. And apparently, they'd already decided what kind of diagnosis they were looking for.

13 WRITE FIRST, SWING LATER

Heather, the occupational therapist, was kind and reassuring. She invited me to the evaluation room, and told me I was allowed to be present throughout the appointment. This was a welcome change from the evaluation process we'd undergone through the school. I settled into a tiny chair along the side, and watched as Heather began her evaluation. Mostly it looked like play. She had a lot of really fun-looking equipment, including a swing that hung from her ceiling. The bottom piece could be changed to make a hammock, a nest, and a number of other things. There were tunnels and balls, bikes and scooters. Thomas seemed to enjoy himself.

At the end of the session, Heather walked us back to the waiting room, and promised her report in two weeks.

"Will your report include a diagnosis? His team

feels that's important." I queried.

Heather answered, "I can diagnose OT issues, but not autism or other brain disorders, if that's what you're asking. I can tell you, that based on what I've read from the school's testing, we'd be willing to offer Thomas a weekly slot for private occupational therapy."

Gratefully, I agreed and stopped at the desk to schedule the appointment. At last, progress.

On the drive home, I asked Thomas what he thought of Heather.

"She has big feet," he noted, "and pretty hair, and I really like her swing." I took this to be an endorsement of sorts, and told him we'd get to go back to see her every week.

"Why?" he asked me.

"Well..." I struggled for the words, trying to draw upon my teaching background, "some kids' bodies are more uncomfortable than others. That's just the way they're made. And Heather knows lots of ways to help your body be more comfortable."

"My body's fine," Thomas replied, "but I'm glad I get play on that swing again!"

Week after week, we made the trek to the center for Thomas's private OT sessions. At first, Heather gave Thomas a lot of leeway, allowing him to choose how to spend his time with her. After several weeks, however, it became clear that she'd gathered enough information to design a therapy program. And that's when things began to go downhill.

"Thomas, come sit in this chair," Heather directed, as we entered the room one morning, "Today, we're going to work on writing."

"I don't want to write. I want to go on the swing!" Thomas replied.

"If you do a good job writing, you can go on the swing for your prize," Heather informed him, "Now come sit down."

Thomas sat in the tiny, straight-backed wooden chair Heather pulled out for him. After making several adjustments, she slid a footstool under the table and maneuvered his legs until his feet rested upon it. Next, she placed a slanted board on the table in front of him, and adjusted the angle. Finally, she handed Thomas a pencil attached to a bright purple bracelet with a dolphin charm. After sliding the bracelet over his wrist, she manipulated his fingers into the standard pencil grip.

"Now, hold the little hanging dolphin with your extra fingers, so they don't cheat." Heather instructed. "Okay, now we're ready to write! Let's start with your name. Do you know all the letters in your name?"

Thomas did. He tucked up one of his legs and leaned forward to begin.

"Oh, no! Not like that!" Heather interjected. She pulled his leg out from under him and rested it back on the footstool. She pushed the chair in and reminded him to keep his back straight.

Thomas tried again. This time he got as far as "T-h-" before Heather interrupted him.

"Uh, oh! Your ring finger is cheating!" she said, "Make him go back down and hold onto the dolphin!"

"That hurts too much," Thomas protested. Watching his little left hand trying to contort itself back into position, I had to agree: it certainly *looked* uncomfortable.

Thomas wrote two more letters. His leg began bouncing up and down as he struggled to form the next letter. Heather stopped him again, reminding him to keep his feet still on the footstool.

Thomas pushed the slanted writing board away and started to get up. "I want to swing now."

Heather was firm. "Not now, Thomas. You have to write all the letters in your name first. Sit down, please."

I saw the look that all mothers recognize. It's the one you see on your child's face just before he loses the battle to resist temptation. Heather, being single and childless, did not recognize it quickly enough. In a flash, Thomas darted away from the table and dove headfirst onto the swing with a whoop of delight.

"Thomas!" Heather's voice was loud and no-nonsense. "You will come back and finish your writing, then you will swing. If you don't come back right now, you'll lose swing for the day."

Defeated, Thomas disembarked and plodded back to his chair. He allowed himself to be molded once again into a proper "ready to write" position. After about 10 minutes, he finally managed to write his name to Heather's satisfaction.

"Good job!" Heather praised him, "Now you can swing."

Thomas hopped on to the swing and Heather pushed him back and forth, round and round. He seemed happy enough. And yet...

Was it just my imagination, or had the spark of joy, the unbridled freedom with which he'd "whooped" earlier, been ever so slightly dampened?

14 INSTINCTS ARISE

From week to week, Thomas's behavior at occupational therapy seemed to deteriorate. I watched as Heather worked with him on things I deemed unnecessary - sometimes even ridiculous. Yet, once again I stuffed down my instincts and tried to be the ever-cooperative parent.

One day, Heather introduced the concept of hand washing. She read Thomas a simple story about a little boy learning to wash his hands. Next, she pulled out several flashcards, each one depicting one of the steps of hand washing. Heather instructed Thomas to put the cards in order. Thomas waffled. I was baffled. I knew he could perform the task. I'd been teaching him proper hand washing technique since he was two years old. Why wouldn't he put the cards in order like Heather wanted?

"Okay, Thomas, let's leave that for a little

while," Heather moved on. "Come over to the sink with me and let's practice washing our hands together." She escorted him across the room to a child-sized sink. There they practiced turning on the water, wetting their hands, and rubbing with the soap. Next, they rinsed carefully, then dried with a paper towel. Finally, the paper towel was deposited in the wastebasket.

"Good job, Thomas!" Heather praised, "Now, let's give those cards a try again. If you can put them in order, you can have three minutes on the swing!"

I sat in my tiny chair, dumbfounded. This was how we were spending our precious OT time? Washing hands? How was this going to help Thomas control his angry outbursts, better slow down his body at bedtime, or alleviate any of the other host of problems I thought we'd be addressing?

But in an instant, I quelled those instinctual questions. They seemed almost heretical. Heather was the professional. If she wanted to spend forty-five minutes on hand washing, then it must be the right thing to do.

On the way out of the building, Thomas stopped to use the bathroom. Not to be outdone by the OT, or perhaps as a sort of penance for my earlier irreverent doubts, I made Thomas repeat the exact process Heather used when it came time to wash his hands. I ignored the look of disbelief he flashed me as he tossed his paper towel into the wastebasket.

The next week, when Heather tried to get him to practice the hand washing routine yet again, Thomas availed himself of his right to civil disobedience. He flatly refused to do what Heather asked.

"Thomas," Heather warned, "remember, if you don't cooperate, you lose swing for the day."

Thomas remembered. But he was unmoved by the threat. He crossed his arms, defiantly refusing to turn on the tap.

"Okay, then, no swing today," Heather proclaimed. At that, Thomas darted around her and jumped into the swing.

"Thomas! Out! Now!" Heather commanded. As she reached for him, he slid off the swing, dashed across the mat, and tried to hide behind my legs.

I was mortified. How *could* he? I couldn't relate on any level. As a child, I always did what teachers told me to do. It didn't matter whether I wanted to or not. All that mattered was pleasing the adults and keeping out of trouble.

I couldn't understand a child who made a different choice. I couldn't, because I didn't understand something much deeper: that Thomas had not yet disconnected from his own inner wisdom. Straying from his own sense of truth just to please an adult was unacceptable to him - and he was willing to endure the consequences.

Heather approached us, and leaned down to speak to Thomas. "Thomas, we can either practice washing hands or we can put the picture cards in order again. You choose."

After a moment, a subdued Thomas emerged. He made his way over to the little table and mechanically began to rearrange the picture cards.

"Can I swing now?" he asked Heather.

"I'm sorry, but you lost swing for today. You can try again next week. Now, let's practice using these scissors." came her reply.

Week after week, I watched Thomas practice skills in OT that seemed unrelated to his issues as I perceived them. Week after week, I witnessed Thomas become sillier and more defiant. Dumbfounded, I watched the now-familiar scenario play itself out - what had started out as a warm, mutual relationship between Thomas and Heather had deteriorated into something colder, more formal, and more authoritative in nature.

My instincts were practically screaming at this point. *"This isn't right! You've got to do something!"* they urged. But how could I stand up to an expert? How could I presume to know better than she? There must be something wrong with me, I decided. A god complex, perhaps. That was far more believable than the alternative: that I knew what my son needed better than all of the professionals I'd met thus far.

But my inner voice had begun to stir from its decades-long sleep. And before long, I was unable to ignore it.

The next week, I summoned up all my courage and asked Heather if we might speak privately for a moment before she began working with Thomas. Heather readily agreed, and giving Thomas some paper and crayons, ushered me outside the therapy room to talk.

"I, um, don't want to presume here, but I've been using a technique with Thomas that really seems to be working. It comes from a book I've been reading. I thought it might be something we could try here in OT when Thomas refuses to cooperate. If you think it's a good idea, I mean." As I described the technique, I silently questioned myself. Why did I feel so tongue-tied and tentative? The girl was clearly a good decade my junior. So why did I feel like a little kid standing up to my teacher?

Heather seemed a bit kerflummoxed. I expect it was a first for her, to be offered advice from a lay person - a mere parent with not a single OT credential to her name. She recovered quickly, though, and consented to give it a try.

Reentering the therapy room, Heather pulled out the schedule and began going over it with

Thomas. As usual, he was very cooperative when it came to his favorite activities. But as soon it was time to do something he didn't enjoy, he became oppositional. He flung his pencil on the floor, marched across the room, and began hiding behind a large gym mat.

"Thomas! Right now it is time to sit at the table." Heather began, then, remembering our agreement, quickly switched gears. She crossed the room and sat cross-legged on the floor in front of him.

"Thomas, I see we have a problem. I want you to practice writing and you want to do something else. Can we find a way to both get a little of what we want?"

"I want to swing!" Thomas exclaimed.

"Oh, I see. You want to swing instead of write."

"Yes!"

"Well, how about this: we swing for three minutes. Then, when the timer goes off, we go practice writing. What do you think?"

"Well...okay," Thomas seemed a bit taken aback. Clearly this was not what he'd been expecting. It was so unlike any of his previous interactions with Heather.

The session seemed to go better after that. But I remained anxious. Did Heather think I was being presumptuous by making such a suggestion? Did she resent me for being right? Or did she secretly think I was dead wrong?

Although I was riddled with self-doubt, I began speaking up more frequently. I requested that Heather focus more on the skills I felt Thomas needed most. I asked for recommendations for books about OT and began educating myself about different techniques and programs. And slowly, my tentative inner wisdom, ignored for so long, began to reclaim its rightful place.

15 WALKING THE SPECTRUM

Autumn packed its bags and abandoned us to the caprice of winter. Thomas's class put on a holiday sing-along just before Christmas break, blending culturally diverse carols with old standbys such as Frosty the Snowman and Jingle Bells. Parents were invited back to the classroom for refreshments.

I'd been in to visit Thomas's class a few times at this point. Each time, I was struck by the way Thomas's teachers seemed to interact with him. There was no gentleness, no light-hearted banter, no playful spontaneity. They spoke in short, direct sentences - loud, slow and clearly articulated. Conversation was very limited. If Thomas tried to wander off topic - or off task - he was firmly redirected.

Where was the relationship? I wondered. I couldn't quite put my finger on it, but something was very wrong. It wasn't that the teachers were *un*kind - but they weren't exactly *kind*, either. The whole thing had an institutional feel about it.

I'd noticed that Heather seemed to interact with Thomas in a similar way during his OT sessions. One morning I broached the subject with her.

"Oh, this is a very common approach to use with kids on the spectrum," she replied. "Language is clear and direct, everything is highly structured and predictable. Boundaries and limits are well-defined and enforced. It works really well for these kinds of kids."

These kinds of kids? I questioned, *What kind, exactly?* And why was Thomas suddenly being treated as one of them? He had yet to be evaluated by anyone qualified to make a diagnosis. So why were his teachers treating him as if he already had one? And what if they were wrong?

I'd seen my share of children on the autism spectrum. Thomas just didn't seem to fit the profile. Maybe it was merely denial, but an autism label just struck a wrong chord deep within me. And there was only way to find out.

Up to now I hadn't felt a sense of urgency to have a label bestowed upon my child. In fact, I was rather relieved that it was going to be quite a while before he could be evaluated. To be honest, I wasn't at all sure I was ready to handle a diagnosis. I was already grieving the loss of my once-perfect child. To be handed a diagnosis would be like being given a death sentence for all my hopes and dreams. My son would be Officially Damaged. The ultimate goal for him would dwindle from a passion-filled, meaningful life to one in which he *might* learn to function independently one day - if we were lucky.

But now, it seemed that a diagnosis was necessary - and sooner rather than later. At our next appointment, I asked Heather if the evaluators' schedules were likely to open up any time soon.

"Sorry, no," was Heather's reply, "we just learned that one of them is retiring at the end of the month, and the other has taken on a professorship. We won't be scheduling new evaluations until September at the earliest."

Heather must have seen the desperation on my face, because her next words were gently spoken, "Don't worry. I've got a colleague who might be able to help. Wait here a moment."

Heather left the room and came back a bit later accompanied by another therapist. She introduced herself and handed me a card.

"This is the name of an excellent evaluator. He's outside our center, and may not be carried by your insurance, but if you let him know I sent you, he'll try to get you in as quickly as possible."

I thanked them both, gathered Thomas up, and

headed to the car. As Thomas began the slow process of buckling himself into his booster, I slid into my seat and studied the card.

Dr. Timothy Marsden, it read. *Pediatric neuropsychologist, specializing in testing and evaluation.* A phone number was listed beneath.

Oh, please, I prayed, *let this Dr. Marsden be our answer. Let him finally get to the bottom of things, so Thomas can start to get better.*

16 VOICES

I called Dr. Marsden's office that very day, and received an appointment for late March - less than 3 months away. I had learned from experience that this was quite a coup. And I was determined to make the most of it. I gathered all of Thomas's information; medical charts, progress reports from both preschools, all testing, and a lengthy history I'd spent hours perfecting. I faxed it all to Dr. Marsden ahead of time. I wanted him to be thoroughly familiar with every aspect of our case before Thomas ever set foot in his office.

Christmas vacation arrived, and with it Thomas's fifth birthday. "Five years old!" I exclaimed as he snuggled into his bed, "How did you get so big?"

"I am big now, aren't I, Mommy?" Thomas answered. "You know what? Now that I'm five, I know I can control myself at school. I just know I can!" I was less confident, but managed to mumble something encouraging before I slipped out into the hallway.

As I shut the bedroom door behind me, I also closed myself off to the possibility that Thomas may be right. And yet within days, I was to see proof of it.

That first week back to school, Thomas transformed himself into an entirely different student. He cooperated and participated. The incidents with Maisie diminished. His teachers were thrilled - finally, some progress! Although I shared the amazing pronouncement Thomas had made to me on his birthday, it was clear that his teachers attributed this progress to something else - their "spectrum" approach.

But this success at school came at an excruciating price. At home, Thomas had reached an all-time low. Thomas was tantruming regularly every school day. His physical aggression had reached new levels. He seemed angry all the time. We all felt like we had to walk on eggshells around him. Heaven help us if we served him juice in the green cup instead of the blue, or handed him his puppy pajamas when he was in the mood for his dinosaur ones. The littlest frustration or disappointment resulted in violent outbursts. The only predictable thing about our days was that Thomas's unpredictability would assuredly lead to a meltdown at some point.

February arrived. Six months had passed since Thomas had started at the integrated preschool. Six months of a downward spiral, leaving me shaken to the core. And finally, having read all the books and tried all the tricks, I grew desperate enough to try something truly radical.

I began to question everything I thought I already knew. I silenced every professional educator, every mainstream expert, every perfectionistic, goal-oriented voice rattling around in my head and listened - really listened - to the only voice left.

That small, shaky inner voice, still so uncertain, cautiously piped up. *"Why are you so set on Thomas completing preschool?"* it asked me, *"Especially when you intend to homeschool him next year?"*

Why indeed? I had no answer except blind fear. Fear that if I tossed out all that professional advice and struck out on my own, somehow Thomas's entire life could be ruined. And it would be all my fault.

Once lent an ear, however, this new voice seemed to gain confidence. *"Thomas doesn't have to stay in preschool,"* it ventured, *"You could withdraw him. How much longer does he need to cry out with his behavior that school is not working for him? When will you listen?"*

Thus began an intense period of self-examination and debate. On the one hand, the new voice, which I had dubbed 'mother's instinct' seemed full of good sense. But the other voices couldn't be completely silenced for long. At times, their arguments were highly convincing. After all, who was I to think I knew more than all of these experienced professionals? How dare I believe I had better answers than they did?

Round and round I went, until that fateful afternoon in early February. Snowflakes drifted lazily out of a mostly blue sky, glittering in the early afternoon sun. Thomas was at school, the twins were asleep, and my mother had popped by to visit. My mind was heavily burdened with this incessant internal dialogue, and I knew from experience that it would help to talk it through with my mom. I shared with her my growing conviction that school was doing Thomas more harm than good, the seedling thought of taking him out, and all of my fears about whether that would be a good decision or an incredibly stupid one.

My mother listened carefully, questioning me now and then, offering her observations when I asked for them.

"Really, Mom, I'm almost convinced that pulling Thomas is the right thing to do," I said. Just then the phone rang. I picked up the receiver and said hello. It was none other than Mrs.

Lambsworth.

"Mrs. Olson," she said, "I know it's a bit early, but are you able to come get Thomas? He's in the principal's office and is too upset to return to class. I don't feel comfortable sending him home on the bus."

I told Mrs. Lambsworth I'd be right there, and ended the call. I could almost see my words still hanging in the air:

"I'm almost convinced that pulling Thomas is the right thing to do"

I turned to my mother. "That was Thomas's teacher," I said. "He's in the principal's office. Now, I'm convinced."

I gathered my coat, my keys, and my courage, and headed out the door.

17 WE'LL TAKE IT FROM HERE

And so, there I sat in the parking lot, trying to martial my resources for what lay ahead. No more waffling. No more trying to be everyone else's version of the perfect parent. It was time to rescue my son.

I drew in one last, shaky breath and made my way into the school, bypassing the principal's office, turning sharply to the right, down the hall that would take me to my son's classroom. *Visitor's pass be damned*, I thought. *I'm done playing by their rules.*

The hallways were empty: school had ended during Thomas's banishment, and all the other kids were happily heading home. I knocked on the classroom door and Mrs. Lambsworth looked up from the table where she was tidying the day's papers. She gestured me over, pulling up a chair opposite hers.

I jumped in before she had a chance to say anything. "Mrs. Lambsworth, I want to thank you for the time you've spent with Thomas. But we both see that this isn't working. My husband and I are going to take it from here."

"You're - you're taking him out of school?" she asked, stunned.

"We are." I had called my husband on the way to the school. None of this was news to him. "Pull him," he'd said, "God knows it's about time!"

"I'm, um, not really sure you can do that, with him on an IEP and all," Mrs. Lambsworth ventured.

"Actually, I can; I've already checked. I just need to sign some papers. I've prepared a letter to his liaison requesting the forms," I replied, holding up an envelope.

It was at this point that Mrs. Lambsworth broke down. "I'm sorry," she whispered, removing her glasses to wipe her eyes, "I feel I've failed you - failed Thomas. I just wasn't prepared to handle the issues that came up. It's been a trying year for me, physically and personally, and I just wasn't up to the challenge." She reached for a box of tissues.

"Mrs. Lambsworth, I know how difficult it's been - for all of us. I really do believe you did your best. But I feel that what Thomas needs now is to be home." My voice was steady. I felt a strange sense of confidence. Finally, *finally*, I was at peace.

"Can we tell him together?" Mrs. Lambsworth asked, dabbing at her cheeks.

"We can," I answered. "Have the principal send him down."

18 WISDOM IN SMALL PACKAGES

I will never forget the next few moments of that day. Thomas arrived, escorted by Mrs. Lee, one of the teacher's aides. He was wearing his red, yellow and blue striped winter coat that was inexplicably reminiscent of a traffic light. His backpack was strapped on. I wondered how long he'd been waiting like that. He looked flushed.

Mrs. Lambsworth thanked the aide, got up from her seat and closed the door. She pointed to a chair next to mine.

"Thomas, would you please sit down here? Your mom and I have something we want to tell you."

Thomas plunked himself down. He looked belligerent. He sat up straight, stiffly indignant, and glared at us.

I took over, "Thomas, Mrs. Lambsworth and I feel that school is not a happy place for you. And we both want you to be happy. So we've decided that you can be all done with preschool. What do you think of that idea?"

Thomas looked perplexed. His gaze shifted back and forth between us as he struggled to comprehend.

"You mean, I can go home now?" he asked after a bit.

"Yes."

"And I can stay home?"

"Yes."

"And I don't have to come back here anymore?"

"That's right."

At that moment, understanding dawned. His entire body slumped with relief. He seemed to let down his guard - perhaps for the first time ever in that classroom.

"Finally," he whispered, almost more to himself than to either of us. "I told you. I told you all along, Mommy, that all I need is to stay with you."

And so he had. For a year and a half, Thomas had been telling me exactly that. He had known instinctually what he needed.

All that time, I'd been striving to fix Thomas, to work within the system, to do what the professionals deemed best. I'd listened to every voice out there but the two most important.

My own instincts.

And my son's.

As it turned out, they were the only ones worth hearing.

19 ANSWERS

A little over a month later, Thomas met with Dr. Marsden for his evaluation. I'd thought about canceling, but a little niggling voice in the back of my head just couldn't let it go. If something *was* wrong, I needed to know. Thomas enjoyed the testing. He'd connected with 'Dr. Tim' right away, counting him among the small group of grown-ups he actually liked. He sailed through the testing and happily informed his new friend that he'd be more than willing to come back any time.

Shortly thereafter, my husband and I met with Dr. Marsden to go over the results. I found myself sitting on the edge of my seat, feeling a bit breathless as we waited for Dr. Marsden to begin.

"Mr. Olson, Mrs. Olson, I've very much enjoyed meeting your son," Dr. Marsden told us in a soft-spoken tone. "As you know, I've spoken to Thomas's special education team at the integrated preschool. At their request, I've evaluated Thomas for autism spectrum disorder, pervasive developmental disorder, and bipolar disorder.

"I've done extensive testing and here's what I can tell you. Thomas does not qualify for any of those disorders at this time."

"I'm sorry," I interrupted, "did you say he does *not* qualify?"

"That's right," Dr. Marsden answered.

It was all I could do to stifle the *"Hah!"* that leaped into my throat at those words. Score one for mother's instincts.

"While he has some qualities that overlap with known symptoms of PDD, I do not believe that is what's going on with your son."

"So, what *is* going on with him?" my husband asked. "Is it a non-verbal learning disorder? ADHD? Dyslexia?" clearly my husband had done his homework.

"Actually, I'm very hesitant to put labels on children," replied Dr. Marsden, "especially ones as young as Thomas."

I began to consider the very real possibility that Dr. Marsden was my hero. Whoever heard of a doctor being *unwilling* to label? My mother's instinct told me we had found someone truly remarkable.

"Here's what the testing tells me," Dr. Marsden continued, "Thomas is an incredibly bright little boy. And, as with most very bright young children, Thomas's intellect far outstrips his emotional maturity at the moment. This can cause a great deal of worry for him. So, *if* I were going for labels, I might mention two: gifted and anxious. They tend to go hand in hand, especially in the early years.

"So, what are my recommendations? It's too early to consider anything as drastic as medication for Thomas's anxiety. I suggest meeting with a counselor - I know a terrific one - and just letting Thomas be himself. Let him recover from the trauma of school, help him to feel safe and secure. In a year, if you feel it's necessary, I can do further testing.

"Bottom line: you've got yourself one very bright, very worried, very wonderful little boy. Take him home and love him. He's going to be okay."

Riding home from that appointment, I felt almost shell-shocked. I'd been prepared to hear almost any diagnosis but that one. *He's going to be okay? Was it truly possible?*

As my husband and I debriefed, I found myself moving from shock to anger. Anger at all of the people who had jumped the gun, labeled my son, and treated him like a "case" instead of a kid. Anger at myself for believing them, and for following their example.

When I'd described the program Thomas's team had been using with him, Dr. Marsden had expressed his disapproval.

"Autism Spectrum Disorder is so prevalent, it's often the first diagnosis teams suspect," he explained, "But this can do more harm than good. For an anxious child, that kind of a program is just about the worst thing you can do. Anxiety-related behaviors can appear to be motivated by defiance and aggression, but they are not. They are motivated by anxiety. And they must be handled very differently.

"When teams use strict boundaries and consequences with an anxious child, it accomplishes nothing but adding to the anxiety, which increases the anxious behaviors. Before you know it, you've created a vicious cycle."

Well, I thought, *that certainly explains a lot*. I'd noticed in his sessions with Heather that the more structured and no-nonsense she got, the worse his behavior became. Now I understood why. What my little boy needed was to feel safe, to feel connected and secure.

It was exactly what he had *not* been getting for more than six months. But that was about to change.

20 HEALING MOMENTS

Spring arrived. As the flowers began to blossom, so did my sweet little boy. He'd been out of school for over two months, and with each passing day I could see a slow but steady recovery. I rediscovered Thomas's smile. When he bestowed it upon me, it was like a ray of sunshine after monsoon season.

Thomas healed and played, played and healed. The days passed quietly, peacefully. Things weren't perfect, but I finally had the sense that the stormy times were on their way out.

One day, out of the blue, Thomas began to talk about his experience at the integrated preschool. As he filled in the blanks for me, a heartbreaking picture took shape.

"Mommy," Thomas said quietly, "Mrs. Lambsworth thought Anthony and I were the crazy dumb kids."

I was taken aback, to say the least. For months, this child had refused to answer a single question about what school had been like. The day he left the building, he'd apparently left behind any intention of ever dredging up the past. Finally, all this time later, Thomas felt safe enough to explore that painful experience.

It all came pouring out: how Mrs. Lambsworth always grouped him with the non-verbal child in the class and kept them with her during any outing. How she spoke kindly to the other children in his class, but spoke sternly to him. How she singled him out when he was part of a group of kids who were misbehaving, sending him out of the room while giving the others a mere warning. The infamous snowball incident - the one that had landed him at the principal's office and had catapulted us into this alternative life - had been just one in a string of interactions that had left Thomas badly damaged.

As Thomas shared, his eyes filled with tears. "I don't know why she hated me so much, Mommy!" he sobbed, "She was so nice to everybody else - I just wanted her to like me, too."

I marveled at how fresh, how raw was Thomas's pain over things that had happened nearly a year earlier. I was wracked with guilt for not pulling him out sooner - for sending him there in the first place - for failing him on so many levels. At the same time, I was filled with gratitude for the learning and growing that had taken place since then. Any doubt I'd had about having done the right thing by choosing to homeschool Thomas vanished in the aftermath of that discussion.

21 READY, SET, HOMESCHOOL

I spent the summer preparing for Thomas's first year of homeschooling. Ever the teacher, I reveled in the planning. I'd turned my perfectionism to a new endeavor: being the best homeschool mother around. After all, I figured, hardly anybody had my set of credentials and prior experience. I could completely tailor the curriculum to Thomas's interests. His kindergarten experience would be the epitome of 'individualized education'.

When it was time to submit a letter of intent to the superintendent, my perfectionism truly peaked. I downloaded the town's curriculum, along with the state's standards and samples from other towns that had excellent reputations. I crafted a document detailing my goals and objectives for each subject, then broke each subject into separate skill areas and wrote more objectives for those. I created tracking sheets to categorize each lesson we did by its subject area and objectives covered.

I was in my element. I knew how to create an education plan from my years of working in special education. Coming up with goals and objectives was second nature. Not to mention that I was fluent in "teacher speak".

I submitted the whole package along with a comprehensive list of my background, certifications and experience. I was certain the superintendent would be impressed.

I felt energized, invigorated. I was super-homeschool-mom! Kindergarten was going to be the best thing that had happened to Thomas. And it was...at first.

22 NEW BEGINNINGS

September. How I loved that slight chill in the early morning air, that turn in the weather that signaled the coming of autumn. September never failed to invigorate me. In my teaching years, August had always felt like a month-long Sunday. September first was like the long-awaited Monday morning. Back to business. September was a new beginning, filled with the promise of a whole new year. Pencils were sharp, notebooks were crisp, everything was new and clean and filled with potential.

And so, that September, I excitedly ushered Thomas into our new "classroom". It had been a playroom before receiving such an illustrious promotion. But over the summer, toys had vacated the premises, and in their place were shelves upon shelves of educational wonders.

Scales, counting bears, pattern blocks and

sorting wheels waited eagerly for math time. Letter people, handwriting books, and phonics programs promised literacy within weeks. Science kits beckoned us to explore magnets, colors, snakes, and volcanoes. A colorful map of the United States and a shelf full of books and videos designed to make history come alive rounded out the social studies section. The walls were decked with posters, charts and an enormous kid-friendly calendar.

As we sat down at the bright blue, child-sized table I'd chosen, I silently congratulated myself. Not only would Thomas and I use this time to reconnect, we'd pursue his education in the best way possible: a curriculum entirely tailored to his abilities. I was certain we were on the road back to happiness.

I think Thomas was willing to give the whole homeschool thing a shot because he, too, was hoping to reconnect - to rediscover that magical, mutual relationship we'd once had so very long ago. But he realized a whole lot sooner than I did that we weren't on the right track. We may have been heading toward the road to happiness but somehow we'd missed the onramp.

For a while, Thomas did everything I asked. When I pulled out the snap cubes, he gamely used them to count how many letters were in our names. When I pointed out the phonics computer program, he grabbed the mouse and started clicking. But his heart wasn't really in it. He wasn't interested in being taught *by* me. What he wanted was to be in a relationship *with* me.

I would read him a book about spiders, and try to get him to write some vocabulary words. He'd start telling silly stories about spiders, hoping to make me laugh. I would encourage him to color his letter people and practice his handwriting. He'd work at a snail's pace, all the while changing the lyrics to the letter songs to include the vocabulary of bathrooms and bodily functions. Thomas was truly puzzled when I declined to join in.

I began to feel impatient; a growing sense of urgency pressing upon me. Didn't Thomas realize that he was getting the ultimate education? Why couldn't he meet me halfway? By gosh, we had a curriculum to follow. And we were falling behind.

To complicate matters further, our fourth child was due the following March. This meant that not only did we need to stay on top of the curriculum, we needed to get ahead of the schedule. I calculated that Thomas and I would need to be at least eight weeks ahead by the time the baby arrived.

Yet, the more I pushed, the more resistance I met. Somewhere in his childish little heart, Thomas realized that we still had a problem. Yes, I had rescued him from the school that had made him miserable. I'd dedicated myself to protecting him - from everybody but me, anyway. But I still had an agenda. I still had something to prove - to myself and everybody else. My connection to Thomas was not my focus. Our relationship was not my focus. Teaching Thomas, and making sure he excelled: that was my focus. Thomas knew it. He felt it. And, thankfully, he rebelled against it.

23 IT TAKES A VILLAGE

Winter arrived. I connected to an online resource and found a local Spanish class for homeschoolers. Of course I jumped at the chance to enroll Thomas. After all, it's a well-established fact that young children are primed for learning a foreign language. I intended Thomas to be bilingual by the time he was a teen. Perhaps he'd even master three languages, if we kept on our toes.

Early in January, Thomas and I drove to the home of another family who'd graciously offered to host the class. It was there that I began to get a taste of what a homeschool community could really be like. Through that family, I became connected to a tightly knit, very supportive group of homeschooling families. There were plenty of opportunities for the kids - and the parents - to build relationships. Holiday events, weekly outings to the park, and various classes promised to keep us busier than ever.

What would have happened, I wonder now, had I not connected with this wondrous group? What twists and turns would my journey have taken? Though I didn't realize it at the time, several of the families I met in this group would point me in a direction I'd never imagined I'd go. A direction, in fact, that I'd never known existed.

Meanwhile, Thomas's anxiety level was still high. He required a tremendous amount of support to make it through the Spanish class or to connect with the other kids at the playground. I began to wonder: what good were all the academics if Thomas was still too anxious to enjoy his life?

One spring morning at the playground, another homeschooling mom and I began chatting about our goals for the following school year. I could hardly believe it when I heard myself saying, "You know, next year, I really just want Thomas to make some friends and learn how to enjoy himself."

Did I really just say that? I wondered, *Me, Miss Teacher of the Year? Did I really just ditch academics for play dates and good times?*

Apparently, I had.

It wasn't until I heard myself make that statement that I realized that somewhere along the way, my thinking had begun to shift. My inner wisdom had found a chink in the armor of my perfectionism, and was beginning to bubble up to the surface. The question was, would I keep listening? Or would I try to patch up that crack in my armor and go back to business as usual?

24 SHIFT

Spring wore on, and our school year wound down. I wrote a detailed progress report and enclosed another laudable letter of intent. An approval from the superintendent's office arrived swiftly. In fact, it came so quickly that I had a niggling feeling that my lengthy missives could not have been read very thoroughly - if at all.

Between the new baby and our many homeschool group activities, I found myself missing "academic" time. I particularly missed teaching math, which had been my favorite. I loved the curriculum we used, and took delight in watching Thomas build his understanding of our number system. In June, I had a brainstorm. I'd open my home to other first graders and run a weekly math class. Thomas would have a social component to his learning, and I'd have a great time playing teacher.

So began "math friends" as it came to be called. Several families joined, and I plunged in wholeheartedly. I looked forward to wearing my teacher hat, to spending time with other moms, and to watching Thomas develop friendships. But, as it turned out, the most important thing about math friends had nothing to do with math at all.

It was through this group that I became acquainted with a small subset of families who were practicing homeschooling in a radically different way. Most of us homeschoolers engaged in "school at home" - there was a curriculum, a schedule, tests, even homework. The location was different, but our kids were still very much steeped in a school model.

As I got to know these families, I discovered that they took an entirely different approach - an approach that took the "school" out of homeschooling. Yes, there was learning going on. But there was no school philosophy. No school mentality. At first, I thought this was decidedly weird - maybe even a bit lazy or neglectful. Certainly not something a former teacher could embrace. Yet, I began to see that these families had a freedom and joy that Thomas and I were missing.

That winter, one of these moms lent me two books. She offered them casually, in a just-thought-you-might-find-this-interesting- kind of way. I didn't know it then, but those books would mark the beginning of a radical paradigm shift.

Over lunch one day, I pulled out the first, a book written by education pioneer John Holt. *How Children Fail*, the title read. Curiosity piqued, I turned to chapter one and started to read.

Two days later, I finished the last chapter. I'd barely been able to put the book down. Holt had described the educational institution as severely limited in its ability to educate children. He discussed the revolutionary idea that *schooling actually interfered with a child's ability to learn*.

I should have been aghast. Here was a man basically taking issue with every educational philosophy and belief I held dear - and yet I couldn't stop thinking about what he'd said. My instincts, growing louder every day, told me that his assertions made sense. Once I was willing to question the status quo, I could see the many flaws in traditional schooling. And I could see how bringing that traditional model into the home could be laden with the same pitfalls.

Slowly, my assumptions and unexamined beliefs were being stripped away. But that left me with a new dilemma. If I gave up school-at-home, with what would I replace it? The answer came in the form of another book - one that would truly change my life.

25 AWAKENINGS

Over the past eighteen months, I'd done exhaustive research about homeschooling. In addition to joining the homeschool group, I had subscribed to several online forums and support groups.

It was there that I first came across the term "unschooling." I'd had no idea what it was, but thought it sounded strange and vaguely fringe-like. Imagine my surprise when I pulled out the second book·my friend had lent me and found that very term emblazoned on the cover.

Radical Unschooling: a Revolution Has Begun, by *Dayna Martin*, it read. I was mildly curious - curious enough to begin thumbing through the book. My eye was drawn to several sentences in bold typeface:

Parenting is supposed to be joyful, and it can be

when we learn to connect with, rather than control our children.

I see my role not as my child's teacher, but as their life and learning facilitator.

Just learning that a new parenting paradigm exists is often the first step in someone's journey to a new awakening.

What?

Parenting being joyful? In my experience, even my best days had been rife with struggle. Managing behavior, minimizing triggers, and raising well-mannered kids had become my major goals, not connecting with my children.

A new parenting paradigm? That couldn't be right. I was pretty sure there were only three parenting approaches: too strict, too permissive, and the parenting program I followed, which was clearly the only correct approach. So where would this new parenting paradigm fall? Would it actually have something valid to teach me?

And what was this about not being my child's teacher? That's *exactly* what I was. Of course, that really hadn't been working out very well, I had to concede.

I flipped the page and came across another bold-face sentence that was certainly bold in its sentiment:

Open your eyes and see how brainwashed we truly are in our culture about what we think education and parenting are.

Excuse me?

I wasn't brainwashed. I was informed, educated, and intentional - wasn't I? I thought back over the course of Thomas's life, all the way back to his infancy. And I was shocked to find the disconnect between what I *felt* and what I *did*.

I remembered moving Thomas into his own bedroom when he was six months old. All the experts said this was important. Babies needed to learn to sleep through the night, to self-soothe, and to get accustomed to sleeping without a parent. But laying in my bed that first night, it took every ounce of self-control not to leap up and snatch Thomas from his faraway cradle. Like the famed Jane Eyre and Mr. Rochester, I felt as though Thomas and I were connected by an invisible cord - one that had stretched too far. I was sure that at any moment the cord would snap and I would, in Mr. Rochester's poignant words, "set to bleeding inwardly." And yet I lay frozen in my bed, squelching that overwhelming instinct to be with my baby. Why, *why* were my actions so divorced from my instincts?

When the girls were born, Thomas had moved into a toddler bed. I scrupulously followed the advice of one of television's all-knowing Nannies in order to get Thomas to stay in his bed. I'd tuck Thomas in and say goodnight. He'd immediately pop out of his bed and flee from his room. I'd pick him up, and following the Nanny's script, utter, "Bedtime, darling!" and carry him back. Thomas would pop out again. This time, and every time thereafter, I'd scoop him up and put him back silently. For *hours*. By the time he'd fall asleep, he'd be frustrated and miserable and I'd be a sweaty, angry mess. No one was happy. And nothing changed. Yet, I was so afraid of spoiling him that I never even considered listening to what his actions were telling me: *'I'm not ready to sleep'* or *'I'm not ready to sleep without you'*.

I thought of the many time-outs I'd enforced when Thomas "misbehaved." I was ever vigilant - for every infraction, Thomas landed in time-out. I believed that those unwanted behaviors must be completely extinguished or I'd have a spoiled brat on my hands - or worse, a juvenile delinquent. But why had I jumped to such extreme conclusions? Well, that's what the popular parenting books threatened would happen. And yet, time-out never seemed to really work. Sure, after a while, Thomas learned to accept going to time-out, but it didn't actually diminish the unwanted behaviors. So why had I kept doing the same thing over and over again, hoping for a different outcome?

I replayed so many Sunday mornings, leaving Thomas in the church nursery despite his pleas for me to stay with him. Everybody knew what to do in that situation: exude confidence, keep it short and hurry out of there. Only the overly-protective, overly-attached mothers hesitated. That's what the veteran moms told me, anyway. And yet, as I confidently made my exit week after week, I felt heart-wrenching pain. *This can't be right*, I'd think. But my thoughts didn't impact my actions. I was too used to setting my own inner voice aside in favor of those I thought were more valid.

Slowly, it began to dawn on me: there were so many areas in which I'd blindly followed the experts: vaccines, fluoride drops, ferberizing, preschool, testing, IEP's, disabilities, therapies... my mind was spinning. Had I ever really thought critically about *any* of these things? The chilling answer was no: I hadn't. I'd read the experts' books, listened to the experts' instructions, and done as I was told. I had silenced my instincts in favor of a more scientific approach.

And look where it had gotten me.

In an instant, it hit me: I was profoundly weary of squashing my instincts so that nobody would think I was coddling my kid, spoiling my son, or parenting permissively. I was sick to death of pretending to be on board with what the experts said. I was exhausted by the burden of fear I carried that if I didn't do everything according to the latest, best research my children would be ruined beyond repair.

I thought of what Thomas had been trying to teach me from the start, with his words and his actions. With every fiber of his being he was communicating this truth:

I'm okay. There's nothing wrong with my body. There's nothing wrong with my mind. I'm a unique, precious being who needs, more than anything, to be connected to you.

It was more true than anything any expert had to say to me. And I was struck with this thought: what amazing things might happen if I started listening to a different set of experts - mother's instinct and child's wisdom?

Dayna Martin's words had proved to be true. Just learning that there was another way to think about parenting had started me on the road to a new awakening.

I was done with status quo, done with consigning myself and my child to expert advice. It was time for a truly radical shift.

26 YOU KNOW, LIKE THE UN-COLA

I devoured Dayna Martin's book about unschooling, then located other books and websites devoted to the subject. So much of what I discovered rang true. Unschooling seemed so in line with what my instincts had been trying to tell me all along.

As it turned out, the term unschooling could be traced back to the very author I'd first read: John Holt. Critical of educational institutions, Holt had begun advocating for a radically different type of education. Its premise was that children do not need to be force-fed facts in order to learn. In fact, he asserted, children learn best when pursuing their own passions with support from the adults around them. Like Sprite, the "un-cola", Holt's version of education was a stand-out alternative to everything else out there.

And it had begun to catch on. At first, it was

rather a small movement, but with the dawn of online forums and blogs unschooling had gained momentum. By the time I started learning about unschooling, it was a well-established sector of home education. Not only was it growing, but it was beginning to make its way into mainstream media.

As a teacher, I found I had a lot of "un-learning" to do about the nature of education. So much of what I'd internalized was being challenged. *Should* all children learn the same thing at the same age? Should the adults decide *what* kids should be learning and *how* they should be learning it? Was it true that learning acquired through pursuing pleasurable activities based in the 'real world' was deeper and better retained than facts and figures learned in class?

In those early days, I clung to one directive: question everything. I began the mental exercise of critical analysis. Every practice, every belief, every fear...I questioned all of it. Sometimes I came out on the other end with a different idea, sometimes not. But my beliefs were always the clearer and more well-defined for having been put through such a process.

As I let go of formal academics, a new world opened up in which I could identify the learning in everything. Whatever we were doing - whether it was playing with a friend, watching a t.v. show, taking a walk or making dinner - I could see it was all rife with opportunities for learning. A profound peace settled over me. I didn't need to concoct a curriculum or craft a list of goals and objectives. Learning would take place naturally, as a side effect of living our lives intentionally and with connection.

Eventually, Thomas noticed our lack of "school time" and commented on it. He could hardly believe his good luck when I described to him what I was discovering about the true nature of learning.

"You mean, we're done with homeschool?" he queried, when I had finished.

"Yup."

"No more on-line phonics or math papers?" he clarified.

"Not unless you're in the mood."

"So we can just...play?" he ventured.

"You've got it."

"Hooray!" Thomas cheered. I joined in.

27 IT'S A WONDERFUL LIFE

At first, Thomas thought there must be a catch. He couldn't believe we could actually just do what we wanted. But after a while we both settled into it. I saw his learning with new eyes, and it was magical. The best part was that I got to be more like Thomas's sidekick and less like his parole officer. We became a team, giddy with our new-found freedom and a slight sense that we were getting away with something. It was thrilling!

The days slipped by as we settled into our new unschooling life. Looking back over the past few months, I was struck at how far we'd come. I thought about what our lives would have been like if we'd followed the traditional path - if Thomas had finished preschool and gone on to kindergarten with a diagnosis, an IEP, and a world of experts dictating his every move.

One evening, Thomas asked me to help him

write a letter to his friend, Sam. I agreed, and we headed to his room to get started.

"Mommy, I want to use the special stationery," Thomas informed me. I retrieved the box and handed it to him.

Thomas perched on his desk chair. His body was precariously balanced on one knee and two elbows as he swiveled the chair back and forth. In teaching, everyone knows that's a red flag. Kids with attention issues tend to sit in strangely contorted ways in order to keep focused. *What would have happened if Thomas were composing this letter at school?* I wondered. I envisioned a morning dose of meds to help him focus, and perhaps a trip to the school nurse after lunch for another dose to get him through afternoon classes.

Blissfully unmedicated, Thomas spent a moment thinking about what he wanted to say to Sam, and then began writing. About three letters into the first word, he stopped and asked me a seemingly unrelated question. I had no idea what meandering stream of thought had led to this, but I answered his question, which touched off a short discussion about the topic. After a few moments, Thomas refocused.

"What next?" Thomas asked himself. "Oh, right."

He continued writing. Sam's letter had been very neatly written. Thomas wanted his letter to be neat as well. He checked with me often about whether a word should be capitalized or if his spacing was adequate.

In all my years teaching, I couldn't remember a student with special needs refocusing himself the way Thomas just had. Usually it was like pulling teeth. And even if I succeeded in dragging the child back from his internal musings, it never lasted for long.

Thomas wrote and asked me a question, wrote and made an observation, wrote and got up to wiggle around. He reminded me of a moth weaving its way through the evening sky looking for its mate: the route seemed ridiculously circuitous, but I knew that eventually the journey would be completed.

I answered Thomas's questions and responded to his comments. I decided to get comfortable, and sprawled out on his rug, my head propped up on his tiny blue couch. As Thomas wrote, I noticed his lefty pencil grip; the one Heather had worked so hard to discourage. He almost never started a letter at the conventional place. *The conventional way to form letters doesn't make much sense from a lefty's perspective,* I reflected. If I were a lefty, Thomas's way probably would have felt more intuitive. That would be beside the point in a classroom, however. At school, there is one proper pencil grip and one proper way to form letters. I could just imagine the look of horror on a teacher's face had Thomas dared to write so rebelliously in class.

After an enjoyable 20 minutes of writing and chatting, Thomas had produced two sentences. Very optimistic, he drew a line about three quarters of the way down the page.

"When my letter is that long, I'll send it," he decided.

Thomas also decided he'd had enough of writing for the time being. Off he went to listen to some music. Two sentences was just fine with me, but I knew it would never fly at school. I remembered my own years as a special education teacher all too well: constantly watching the clock, trying to motivate my students to pick up the pace. If all else failed, we stayed in for recess or skipped free reading time in order to play catch up.

The next evening before bed, Thomas pulled out his letter. "I'm determined to finish this tonight, Mommy!"

We settled down, me on the rug again, Thomas on his swivel chair using a rickety end table as a desk. We chatted as he wrote. Something he had heard at play rehearsal came up again and again, until finally he giggled, "Boy, Mommy, that really tickles my fancy!" and we burst out laughing. I could see Thomas needed to use the bathroom, but he was too into his writing to take a bathroom break. I had to promise him he could come right back and keep writing before he consented to go. He was there and back in record time.

I couldn't help but remember the infamous bathroom breaks of my teaching days. I knew exactly how this one would have gone if Thomas had been writing the letter for a school assignment. Having been coerced to write more than he wanted to, and forced to sit in an uncomfortable position, Thomas would have been desperate for an escape. Like multitudes of children before him, Thomas would have availed himself of one of the few options left to him: a hasty retreat to the boys' room.

After half an hour Thomas still showed no sign of slowing down. *I* was the one getting tired, and I asked him if we could wind it up. Although we agreed on a few more minutes, at least fifteen passed before we actually finished. At long last, Thomas wrote his final sentence, signed his name, and triumphantly danced his way over to me.

We marveled for a moment at this accomplishment, speculated on how excited Sam would be to receive it, and wondered when to start checking our own mailbox expectantly for a reply.

As I tucked Thomas into bed, I felt a rush of

gratitude for this life we'd discovered - and for the suffering and frustration we'd so narrowly escaped. I celebrated the joy I saw on my little boy's face, the laughter we had shared, and the moments of truly authentic collaboration.

I was amazed at the way unschooling had changed so much about our lives. Like the old film classic, *It's a Wonderful Life*, I could almost see the path we didn't take, and where it would have led.

And I thought to myself, *Jimmy Stewart's got nothing on us*.

28 EMBRACE WHO YOU ARE

Over time, I discovered that a different way of looking at education was only the tip of the unschooling iceberg. At its core, I learned, unschooling was about connectedness, mutual respect and trust. Trust that children learn what they need to know in order to follow their passions. Trust that, with support and gentle guidance, children are able to accomplish truly great things.

Radical unschooling extended this trust into many aspects of a child's life: respecting his food choices, or helping her to find her own sleep rhythm, for example. Not to mention treating our kids with the same respect we demand they show us.

My husband and I found that the more we were able to practice this philosophy, the more peaceful our household became. Thomas grew secure in his knowledge that we were on his side. We were a team, working together to honor everybody's needs and wishes. Finally, *finally*, he knew he was going to be heard.

But it wasn't always an easy road. Mainstream voices had a way of creeping back inside my head, trying to re-establish residence. This was especially true, I discovered, when it came to gender stereotypes.

Although Thomas had outgrown his earlier preference to be a girl, he still liked to play "girl" games with "girl" toys. When friends and family asked for his Christmas or birthday list, I'd cringe inwardly at his requests. Mermaid costumes, My Little Pony figurines and doll house furniture topped his list. No toy guns or baseball gloves for him, thank you.

Clothing was another uncomfortable arena. Thomas was drawn to "girl" fashions. He preferred pink and purple fabrics decorated with flowers or stars. Sometimes he even expressed a wish for a nightgown or skirt like his sisters wore.

Thankfully, I was able to hear my inner wisdom at this point. I was (mostly) convinced that Thomas's choice of toys and clothing had much to do with his siblings. Still, it took me a while to become courageous enough to allow Thomas the freedom and acceptance he so eagerly desired.

One day, as we prepared for an outing at the

park, Thomas retrieved an old, flowered sunhat and announced that he wanted to wear it instead of his baseball cap.

My mother and I exchanged glances. A flowered hat in the back yard was one thing. But at a park full of kids who may not be as, well, *accepting* as one would like? That was a horse of a different color.

I hesitated. Voices raged inside me, doing battle. What would the parents think of me? What would the kids think of Thomas? What would they say - or do? Painful scenarios flitted across my mind's eye.

In the end, though, I couldn't justify refusing him. Nodding, I told Thomas that he was welcome to wear the hat. "But," I cautioned, "the kids at the park might wonder why you're wearing it. Have you thought about what you might say if somebody asks you why you're wearing a girls' hat?" I felt I owed it to Thomas to give him a heads-up and help him prepare an answer should such questions arise.

As it turned out, Thomas needed none of my help. Although he seemed mildly puzzled as to why anybody would think of it as a girl's hat to begin with, he had his answer ready. "Well, that's easy, Mommy," Thomas replied, "I'll tell them I'm wearing it because I like it."

And so he did. We hadn't been there five

minutes when a true "boy's boy" approached and asked Thomas why on earth he was wearing a flowered hat. Thomas's response was so authentic, so confident, that the boy simply accepted it with a shrug of his shoulders and a quiet, "Oh." Then he invited Thomas to join him on the monkey bars.

Once again, my son's inner wisdom had taught me a priceless lesson. But I still had much left to learn.

It took me a long time to truly make peace with Thomas's personal preferences. My actions predated my feelings. Long before I was really "okay" with it, I began allowing Thomas the freedom to choose clothes of either gender. I'll never forget his first nightgown. Purple, with fat pink and blue polka dots, it matched the one his sister Faith had chosen moments before. Thomas put it on and spun around enthusiastically. The joy that garment brought him was plain to see. But as I slinked up to the counter to pay for it, I found myself praying that the clerk wouldn't figure out I was buying the nightgown for him.

Another time, Thomas was adamant about wearing a skirt to church. Church, of all places! *Why*, I begged him silently, *why must you require this kind of a stretch from me? Please, please, anywhere but church!*

But I took some deep breaths and acquiesced.

Thomas ended up pairing the skirt with a pair of pants and a long shirt, and most people never even noticed. Still, what was important was that I was learning to value Thomas's intrinsic joy at freely expressing his sense of style over what other people might think of him - or me.

Over the course of time, I came simply to see *Thomas*, rather than a boy dressed embarrassingly like a girl. I learned to appreciate his uniqueness and marvel at his bravery. He was exactly who he was. Totally authentic and at ease with himself. It was truly inspiring.

And then he met Peter.

29 A PAIR OF SPARKLY SNEAKERS

Thomas and Peter became fast friends the summer Thomas turned eight. Peter was a rather surprising playmate; he and Thomas were polar opposites in many respects, especially when it came to clothing. Peter loved sports, and most of his clothes sported the logos of one team or another. His footwear was a testimony to super heroes and action figures. He was about as "boy" as it gets.

Most of the time, this didn't seem to bother either one of them. But as the summer wore on, I overheard Peter questioning Thomas about his love of all things "girl".

Although Thomas's responses seemed self-assured, this first experience with a good friend questioning his choices began to take a toll. This became painfully apparent the day Thomas and I went to the shoe store to get him a new pair of sneakers.

Entering the store, we headed over to the boys' section. Thomas glumly surveyed the offerings.

"They're all black, white or blue, Mom," he lamented, "and the only decorations are super-heroes. It's so not fair; the girls get all the fancy stuff!"

He had a point. The girls' section across the way was at least twice as large as the boys' and sported a whole host of colors and designs.

The meager pickings in the boy' section left Thomas discouraged and uninspired. He had wanted a pair of sparkly sneakers, something fancy, something eye-catching, something that danced on his feet.

In earlier days, I would have pointed out the snazzy bright red Spiderman sneakers, or the wow-factor of the soles that lit up with each step of the black pair. Ill at ease, I would have tried to talk Thomas into a non-controversial pair of shoes. Something solidly in the masculine camp. But not that day.

"You're right, Thomas," I said, as I steered him over to the girls' section, "Let's see what we can find over here."

I could feel him searching my face as I turned my attention to finding his size. *Is this really okay?* he seemed to be asking.

I pointed to several different styles. "So, any of

these catch your eye?" I asked him. *Yes, this really is okay*, I tried to communicate.

I sensed the tension drain from Thomas's body. He let out a big breath and began perusing the sneakers. His eyes came to rest on a gorgeous pair, sort of a pastel bluish-purple infused with strands of silver. They fit perfectly.

For a moment, Thomas was thrilled. Then his eyes clouded with misapprehension. "What will Peter say?" he worried.

There, in the shoe aisle, we had a brief but heartfelt discussion.

"Before you can decide whether to purchase these sneakers," I told him, "you must decide whether it is more important to wear something that brings you joy or to wear something that meets with your friend's approval."

Thomas wanted to know my opinion about the sneakers. "Do *you* think I should get them, Mommy?"

"I hope you'll listen to what your own heart is telling you, Buddy, not mine or anybody else's."

After a moment's hesitation, he informed me that he wanted the sneakers. "After all, I can always wear my old boyish ones around Peter," he added.

How different would this trip be, I wondered, if Thomas had still attended school? If he'd been rubbing shoulders with multitudes of kids who questioned and ridiculed his choices? How would the constant pressure to conform have affected him? Would he have risked being teased? Or would he have walled off parts of himself, those essential but "uncool" pieces of his precious soul? How long would it have taken before that spark of joy I loved to behold in him flickered and died?

I reflected on our group of homeschoolers and unschoolers: a wildly varied lot. We were a motley but lovable crew; some boys with short hair, some with long. Some with ordinary names, others graced with names that sang of other times and places. Some boys who played with trucks, and some boys who knitted (and some who enjoyed both), and even some who wore a pair of flowered pants now and again when the mood struck. They were mostly like any other group of kids, but with one crucial difference. This bunch had learned the inestimable quality of acceptance. They may not all have been best friends. They may have gotten on each other's last nerve every so often, but almost never did they question another's right to be just who he or she was. It was really pretty glorious to behold, and I breathed out a silent prayer of thanks that we had been brought into communion with such wise and wonderful little people.

Later that afternoon, Peter showed up at the door, wanting Thomas to go out and play. Two pairs of sneakers - one old, and one new - lay strewn on the floor of the foyer. Thomas sat down and put on a pair. The new pair.

Sparkle on, my boy, I thought to myself, smiling, *sparkle on*.

30 LIVING THE SPARKLY LIFE

A year has passed since that day at the shoe store. The sparkly sneakers, worn thin from use and far too small, have been replaced by a trendy new pair. But much more than Thomas's shoe size has changed.

At nine and a half, Thomas is flourishing. The boy who literally couldn't spend five minutes apart from me at age five now enthusiastically takes on new challenges at every turn. He just performed in his ninth musical, this time in a leading role. He is a gifted artist, a whiz of a mathematician, and an insect enthusiast.

He's also a tiny but powerful advocate for unschooling. Having lived in both worlds, Thomas is in a unique position to compare and contrast. In 2010, our family had the privilege of working with internationally recognized unschooling advocate, Dayna Martin. Thomas connected deeply with her simple yet profound wisdom and her peaceful, loving spirit.

To this day, when an unsuspecting adult makes an innocent remark about school, Thomas pounces on the opportunity.

"Oh, I don't go to school," he always begins, "I'm unschooled. It's a kind of homeschooling where you learn by doing what you love. If you have any questions, just ask my friend Dayna. She can tell you all about it!"

All he needs now is a business card.

This past week, we bumped into a homeschooling mom who hadn't seen Thomas in several years. Extremely comfortable with adults, Thomas chatted with her amiably for a few minutes before zipping away to play with his sisters. My friend looked at me incredulously. "This is not the boy I met three years ago," she exclaimed, "I can't believe the change!"

Indeed. My sweet, gentle, funny, brilliant boy has come out of hiding. Gone are the explosions, the inexplicable behaviors, the crippling anxiety. He is living a life of freedom, and I believe it has truly saved his life. Is he perfect? Of course not. As he told Ted after he'd lost his temper one afternoon and whacked his sister, "Daddy, you know I'm still a work in progress." As are we all.

Our family continues to tread the exhilarating path of radical unschooling. It has been an exciting, inspiring journey. There have been bumps in the road and rough patches along the way. But both the successes and the struggles have left us stronger, more connected, and more sure of our direction.

I see so many mothers today struggling the way I did all those years ago - trying to do everything right, trying to raise well-behaved kids, listening to so many experts and so much advice that their heads are spinning. They're filled with fear that the mistakes they make will be insurmountable. Like I once did, they have silenced their mother's instincts and hushed the childish words of wisdom lisped by their little ones. Each day the disconnect grows greater and greater, until one day, they will forget those voices ever spoke at all.

But it doesn't have to be that way. If we can remember to hold the advice and opinions of others lightly, to leave space for our own answers to bubble up from deep within our hearts, and to truly listen to what our children tell us - both with their words and their actions - we can reconnect. We can be as deeply bonded with our children as when we held their tiny forms for the first time and marveled at the sheer wonder of their presence. We can recapture the joy in the journey, rather than gritting our teeth and trying to make it to the finish line, only to discover that in our frenzy to succeed as parents, we missed the point entirely.

As I look back over the years, I find I am filled with unspeakable gratitude for my amazing little boy. The teacher in me humbly acknowledges that the life lessons he has taught me are of far greater worth than the packaged curriculum I once foolishly tried to foist upon him. His authenticity, his tenacious refusal to settle for the ordinary and unexamined, and his depth of wisdom challenge and inspire me daily. Sparkly shoes or not, Thomas's entire being glitters and glows, and I am truly dazzled.

SHE LET GO

She let go.
Without a thought or a word, she let go.

She let go of the fear. She let go of the
judgments.
She let go of the confluence of opinions
swarming around her head.
She let go of the committee of indecision within
her.
She let go of all the 'right' reasons.
Wholly and completely, without hesitation or
worry, she just let go.

She didn't ask anyone for advice.
She didn't read a book on how to let go.
She didn't search the scriptures.
She just let go.
She let go of all of the memories that held her

back.
She let go of all of the anxiety that kept her from moving forward.
She let go of the planning and all of the calculations about how to do it just right.

She didn't promise to let go.
She didn't journal about it. She didn't write the projected date in her Day-Timer.
She made no public announcement and put no ad in the paper.
She didn't check the weather report or read her daily horoscope.
She just let go.

She didn't analyze whether she should let go.
She didn't call her friends to discuss the matter.
She didn't do a five-step Spiritual Mind Treatment.
She didn't call the prayer line.
She didn't utter one word. She just let go.

No one was around when it happened.
There was no applause or congratulations.
No one thanked her or praised her.
No one noticed a thing.
Like a leaf falling from a tree, she just let go.

There was no effort. There was no struggle.

It wasn't good and it wasn't bad.
It was what it was, and it is just that.

In the space of letting go, she let it all be.
A small smile came over her face.
A light breeze blew through her.
And the sun and the moon shone forevermore.

Ernest Holmes

AN INTERVIEW WITH THOMAS

In the story, most of Thomas's comments reflect what he was thinking and feeling during his early years. In the course of writing this book, Thomas and I have had many conversations about that time in his life. It's been enlightening to revisit that period in our family's history, and to hear Thomas's perspective all these years later. Below are excerpts from some of those conversations.

What do you remember about the integrated preschool?

I remember sitting in the corner sometimes. I missed recess and got sent to the principal's office.

I felt trapped. I missed Mommy. School felt like a controlled house with a mean mother. I wanted to run away but Mrs. Lambsworth wouldn't let me.

When I came home, I just wanted to punch my mom in the face for sending me to that stupid school.

How would you describe your teacher, Mrs. Lambsworth?

Mrs. Lambsworth didn't know me, didn't seem to understand what I wanted or when I had a problem. All she would do was hold me in from recess instead of trying to help me work it out.

She never smiled. She didn't like kids. She'd lock eyes with you and scream at you, even when you were sweet - like I was (even though I didn't seem that way).

So what was really going on with you and Maisie?

Maisie was nice. I was partners with her once. I used to like to mush Katy. I liked to mush Maisie, too. Mrs. Lambsworth used to yell at me. She would say in a loud, angry voice, "Hey, stop that, that's personal space!"

What do you remember about the day you were sent to the principal's office for throwing snowballs?

Other kids started throwing the snowballs, but only I got sent to the principal because Mrs. Lambsworth just hated me. She *especially* hated me. And I hated her. It was like two pigs in a pigpen who were enemies. Only Mrs. Lambsworth was more of a warthog.

How did you feel when you heard that you didn't have to go back to preschool?

When Mommy said she'd finally take me out, I was so happy! It was probably the only time I ever smiled at school. I couldn't wait to yank her out of the room forever. I never wanted to go back.

What did you think about the time you spent with Heather?

She was supposed to help me have more fun, but I think that description was a lie, because she spent most of her time getting me ready for school. She only gave me 5 minutes a day doing what I liked to do, and the rest of the time she made me do work. I didn't like that, and it wasn't why I was there. I felt like I was in a small little cage.

What did you think of homeschooling?

I thought I'd be happy when my mom took me out of preschool and homeschooled me, but I felt something just wasn't right. I needed to learn for me.

When my mom made me do homeschool, every day I had to pick a subject to learn about. I wanted to play with her - *play*. And I do up until this very moment.

Talk about unschooling. How would you describe it?

The other day, I found a grasshopper and I wanted to look it up. That's what unschooling is. Unschooling is learning by playing. Like when we got butterflies and we watched them and looked them up. We didn't just go in a classroom and start learning about them.

In school you learn what they want. It's boring and you forget. At home, you learn what you want. Kids are in school six hours a day, but I'm learning all day. Unschooling goes on - it never ends.

The truth is, you're already learning - no matter what you do, you're learning.

What advice would you give to parents?

Unschooling is a great way to learn. I encourage you to try unschooling. Consider stopping giving workbooks and let your kids do what they want because the more you want to do it, the more you have fun learning it.

With unschooling, you'll be able to watch your kid learn and grow. It may be hard at first, but you can look up unschooling - there are lots of good descriptions of it.

It's a really fun way to learn, and happy, so your kids will have a happy life.

MORE ABOUT UNSCHOOLING

Asking, "What is unschooling?" is a little bit like asking, "What is love?" or "What is happiness?". It means different things to different people. But within its broad framework, there are some fairly consistent themes and basic beliefs that most unschoolers embrace.

Belief #1: Children are hard-wired to learn.

By nature, children are curious and passionate about exploring. In The Magic Years, author Selma Fraiberg uses the term, "infant scientists". Children are constantly exploring their world, testing their discoveries, and drawing conclusions. Play is a primary vehicle for these explorations, not only in the early years, but for older children as well.

Belief #2: When one is interested in something,

learning takes place.

Think about what you've learned in your adulthood. What do you know a lot about? Most likely it's the stuff you've stumbled across that really interests you. My husband developed celiac disease, and needed a gluten-free diet. I wanted to understand his condition, and support his dietary changes. Because of my interest, I soaked up information about the topic in every way I could. I read about it, talked to others with the condition, found cookbooks, watched videos, etc. It did not feel like a chore. It was fascinating. And I didn't need anyone assigning me texts, asking me to write essays, or drilling me with quizzes in order to motivate me to acquire the information. ·

Belief #3: Learning is a side effect of playing, pursuing interests, and developing passions.

Learning is not the goal itself; it is a by-product. For example, a toddler gains a large vocabulary so that she can better be understood by those around her. She does not wake up one morning thinking, "Gee, I'd really love to know at least 500 words by the time I'm three. I'd better get busy!" The vocabulary is a means to an end: being able to communicate efficiently. Reading is another example. No one learns to read simply for bragging rights (Learn to read: check! Done with the written word!). No, we learn to read because it is a means to an end, whether that end be enjoying a good story or being able to figure out which button to click in order to print. Reading allows us access to information, which in turn allows us to pursue our interests more efficiently.

Belief #4: Parents are not teachers

A child may learn something from – or in spite of- the adults in his world, but learning is centered within the child himself. Learning is not the result of teaching; therefore parents should not focus on being teachers. Instead, the parent's role is to closely connect with the child, noting his/her interests and then providing opportunities for the child to pursue that interest. This does not mean designing an integrated unit on spiders for a kid who's into bugs (let's count the legs, let's learn how to spell spider, let's read a book about them!). Instead, the parent brings as much as possible into the child's world to support that child's passion – however long-lasting or brief it may be. This may mean borrowing books and videos, setting out a magnifying glass, or capturing that hairy guy on the ceiling in a glass jar instead of squishing it…get the idea?

Unschooling was first coined by author John Holt back in the 1970's. It was meant to connote an alternative to schooling, just as Sprite soda was the "un-cola" – an alternative to Coke or Pepsi. There are dozens of other phrases used to describe this type of homeschooling, and each one focuses on a certain aspect of it. Here are some examples: delight-driven learning, child-led learning, interest-led learning, fun-schooling, life-experience learning, relaxed homeschooling, child-centered learning, passion-driven learning.

And finally, my own description: Unschooling is a child-led, adult supported, passion-based way of life.

RESOURCES

Books:

The Explosive Child, by Ross W. Greene

The Highly Sensitive Child, by Elaine N. Aron

How Children Fail, by John Holt

Radical Unschooling: A Revolution Has Begun, by Dayna Martin

Raising Your Spirited Child, by Mary Sheedy Kurcinka

Siblings Without Rivalry, by Adele Faber & Elaine Mazlish

On the Web:

unschoolers.org: Nicole Olson's official website

psychologytoday.com/blog/freedom-learn: Dr. Peter Gray

naturalchild.org: The Natural Child Project

joyfullyrejoycing.com: Joyce Fetteroll

daynamartin.com: Dayna Martin

ahaparenting.com: Dr. Laura Markham

ABOUT THE AUTHOR

An unschooling mother of four, Nicole Olson is the voice behind the internationally recognized blog unschoolers.org. Nicole holds dual certifications in regular and special education and taught in a variety of capacities and grade levels before becoming a full-time mom. Recently, she has combined her passion for unschooling and her love of writing to author a series of children's books about radical unschooling, due out in spring, 2013.

Made in the USA
Charleston, SC
11 November 2012